Life
in a
JIFFY

Life in a JIFFY

Short Poems and Fiction Stories

SAM

PARTRIDGE
A Penguin Random House Company

To order additional copies of this book, contact
Partridge India
000 800 10062 62
www.partridgepublishing.com/india
orders.india@partridgepublishing.com

ABOUT THE AUTHOR

Born on 12 January 1987, Sameera spent a good part of her life in IRMA Campus in Anand, Gujarat after her early childhood in Hyderabad and Warangal in Andhra Pradesh, India. A graduate in electrical engineering and a post graduate in management, she started her work life in Mysore and continued in Bangalore as Business Analyst with Software Paradigms Infotech.

Sameera and her loving husband Sanjay died on their way to Waynad in an unfortunate road accident on 01 Novemeber 2013 near famous Ponkuzhy Temple in Kerala barely three months after celebrating first anniversary their marriage on 28 July 2013. This compilation from her blog Life-in-a-Jiffy is brought out by Manasa, elder sister of Sameera and bereaved parents of Sanjay and Sameera.

(c) Kamal Aakarsh Vishnubhotla

(c) Kamal Aakarsh Vishnubhotla

FOREWORD

Sameera Kesiraju, the author, was a nature lover and a very optimistic writer. She was enjoying every bit of nature since childhood and like every other kid, loved to pen down her thoughts. Time passed, seasons changed but the fondness towards writing by crafting all her thoughts and emotions into words on paper grew deeper. Reading every single page of this book will definitely give you a crisp and fresh artistic outlook on life, nature and many of your beliefs. The author has sprinkled nectar of freshness in her writings through very simple and creative poetry.

The poems are so beautifully written that you can connect yourself with every emotion of life and relate to soul touching experiences. This is not just true about poems but you can also taste the beauty of feelings that revolve in our everyday life in shape of short fiction stories. She also chiseled the emotions, activities and minor details of day to day life in a wonderful manner which will definitely make the reading an experience in itself.

She wrote about herself:

> I can't put a label,
> I can't define,
> I can't describe in words,
> That is what I am,
> I am much more than I let you know,
> I love to stay undefined, yet
> I am a mere thought,
> I am just an image of a mind.

Sameera continues to remain (not) a mere thought and (not) just an image of a mind to the many, like us, who were touched by the magic wand of her forever transforming presence.

That Day

That 'that day', was the most wonderful day
That day, I had smiled probably my most
That day, 'he' and me were deliciously close
That day, a warm Sunday, we had indulged with chocolate and pie
That day, we had walked our dog, under the rainbow sky
That day, I had wondered, "Could this be the best I'd lived to see?"
That day, I had believed there was no better place where I could be.
That day, when the sun had finally drowned,
That day, had become that 'better place' where,
I could always be.

~Sam

Wednesday, May 29, 2013

An Evening Conversation

Every evening is a conversation,
Sun's retiring talk with a dear tree
"I'll come in the morn looking for you!
I'll knock on the doors of darkness with a request
To let my rays caress with love, your gentle leaves
As they swing with joy, with hope, to see another dawn
Waiting for me to bring *that dawn* to you
I'll come, but promise that you will not let . . .
The black dusk swallow it all up—every time I am gone."

~Sam

Intervals of longing

There are these intervals,
Intervals that appear out of nowhere,
Intervals that suddenly fill in the gaps

Gaps, between those minuscule measures of time,
Gaps that never made their presence felt ever before,
Gaps that are now, eternal moments of longing

Longing to feel your warmth,
Longing to touch your face,
Longing to let each of my heartbeat become
a witness of your presence,
Because somewhere away . . . you too are caught,
Caught in the same longing that those intervals bring,
Caught in those intervals that appear out of nowhere.

~Sam

Pensive Mood

In a pensive mood she stands, staring at the blank walls
There is so much on her mind,
Do not disturb her,
As she entangles herself in intricate thoughts
As the clock strikes twelve,
She watches the second hand move,
From one melancholic day into another
Will this day be any different? She wonders
Will the hollow fill itself as the minutes pass?
Or will she be stuck even today,
Without knowing the difference in the present and the past

~Sam

A cup of ecstasy

Unabashedly it flirts with my senses

As my hand wraps around it, lifting it in the air

Its aroma promises a ghastly affair

I will indulge, give in, I have no win, I am aware

Yet, I let it slip through my lips, onto my tongue

Little spice and a bit bitter, I feel deliciously numb

To the ecstasies of, a hot cup of chocolate

Oh! Who didn't succumb!

~Sam

A Perfect Blossom

When life gets tough

Many submit to it—fail and succumb

Lose track of desires and become numb

Few count on their stars to treat them fair

Some join their palms; plead the Lord with a prayer,

But have faith, it is there, in your life and in mine too,

Like it is in the life of every cherry tree that ever grew

Forge ahead with your will, be deaf and blind

You are an element of the nature,

Bear that, in mind!

A Perfect Blossom

That's your destiny defined!

~Sam

Charming Phase

It is not the mornings, it is not the night

It is in that lull when the dark aches to turn bright

Words dance on my tongue, and, your ears merrily tune

May be it's that, that, charming phase of the moon

~Sam

Explore the sail

From one shore to another we move,
Only to meet each other midway
Each one has traveled—half the distance,
Yet a new ocean lays bare
We can either drop the anchors,
And talk about the journey so far made
Or we can tie our boats together,
Explore the sail, till the shores fade . . .

~Sam

Tuesday, July 3, 2012

Beautiful broidery

As the sunlight cascades down
And, day drowns in the golden mellow

Bring with you, some words of yours
While I bring with me, some prose of mine

Let us befriend the soul each one holds
Push open, the doors, of our concealed worlds

Charming, wouldn't it be? What awaits a discovery?
Conversations, spinning a beautiful broidery.

~Sam

Come Away

Come away; walk with me beneath the lilac bloom
Come away; skip the routine, it will merrily resume
Come away; for the sun shines bright and high now
Come away; for time is ripe, few words we need to sow
Come away; see the colours, hearts have mischievously spread
Come away; let conversations stray, in the said and unsaid
Come away; for the emotions dance with the swirl of the breeze
Come away; for a stroll, for a moment of ease.

~Sam

Blooming joy

It waited for seasons to turn around
When its leaves shed, it was barren and brown

Through the breezy winters and sprinkles of rain
To the days when sun frolicked in its warmth again

With the first ray of the summer dawn
It swayed in its beautiful yellow gown

Bud to flowers not one but many
A full bloom, a joy, as sweet as honey!

~Sam

Tuesday, February 21, 2012

"Who are you?"

Don't talk about what the world made of you!
Show me your insanity.
Shut your eyes. Be blind.
Be innocent. Have faith.
I am not the world—I am me!
Let's start again, "who are you?"

~Sam

A tacit romance

Words will never have that artistry,
The artistry of a lingering glance,
And, speech can never capture the nuances,
The nuances and the elegance of a tacit romance!

~Sam

Simple Man

"I am a simple man" you tell me
And you ask, "What about me, do you adore?"
You being oblivious about the darling you are
It makes me fall for you, each day, a little more!

~Sam

Well, I haven't been around for a while.
I have hearty news to share.
I ~~am~~ getting engaged this Feb 29th (No kidding, this is a leap year) Yay!
Many good friends I know are shocked out of their wits!
One even asked me," What the hell happened to you?
What's wrong?" Nothing . . .
I just happened to meet a guy I couldn't say no to and in fact said yes,
with delight.

Kiss the ground

The fresh breeze kissed my skin,
The greenery caressed my soul,
Shimmering water greeted the early morn,
In a breath of air, I took it all!
Where ever I be tomorrow
In my heart it will be—this miraculous dawn
In a moment it bounded me eternally
Makes me want to bend down—kiss the ground!

~Sam

P.S: I love this city so much!

Let life surprise you

What is that prudent planning you do?
You think life won't surprise you?
When it does,
Let it amaze and nourish your soul,
Be it joy, pain or grief—embrace it all!
Remember, you are a wave of the ocean,
Where else can you float, but to the shore?

~Sam

Choices

"Be careful", they say
"Be wary of the choices that you make"
Aye foolish souls!
Haven't you known, it yet?
It is the same life whichever path you take!

~Sam

Come unprepared

It is easy to be charmed,
So effortless, to let the heart stray,
But, come talk to me on a darker day
See me in the blackest of moods
Let me wander—detached and alone
Follow me if you have the heart to
Come unprepared, into my life
See the brightest day, the deepest night
Don't catch me when I fall
Fall with me gracefully, touch the ground
Then name yourself mine, and, I'll term myself yours.

~Sam

Carolina..

There is subtle tease,
In the whiff that lingers, after you leave
It is your scent that turns sublime desire wild
Alluring and soothing, like a lovely old wine
Intoxicated, you leave me, wishing you were mine!

~Sam

P.S: I did buy it. ;)

At First Sight!

There is sudden charm around me
When I catch your glancing eyes
I feel beautifully young and bold,
Yes, that's the feeling precise

When you walk towards me,
Futile, my effort of thinking twice
I could toss my world aside
To be enticed and to entice

When you pause to catch a breath,
Weigh your words before they fall
You make me feel precious
I am such a girl after all

As we stand beside each other,
With a million thoughts on our mind
We both are wishing the same-love,
"I wish you could be mine!"

~Sam

Tell me something about you

How naïve can you be, when you ask-
Tell me something about you dear,
How foolish is that, not to know,
Merely lending an ear is not how you hear

I will still tell you, that I lived twenty four,
Already changed like a million fold,
Little different I am each time,
Each time, my feet touch the floor

But, if you want to persist, pursue this goal
Be a friend, a friend till I am trembling old
And that's only way will hear my dear,
Something about me—without being told!

~Sam

Uncertainties

(c) Ashish Arora Photography—Used with permission

I can only see as far my sight,
My mind is made up; I am ready for the flight,
Over the hills, I will fly, into the open skies
The reflection of the world, I will behold in my eyes

Too young, they tell me, what do you know?
These wishes are pointless, someday you will grow.
Uncertainties will ground you, like these pebbles, under your feet,
I am sorry, my child, someday, destiny you shall meet.

They say, I might be left gloomy and teary-eyed,
But what if, I make it, to the other side?
Let the fate come find me, somewhere on the path
At least, I can pride, I had braved a start.

-Sam

P.S: This was written as a part of Captured writings.

Camera Crazy

Twice I had kept aside a thirty grand
Saving rupee by rupee, clutched in my hand
I longed to wear that Nikon strap around neck
Have a SLR that shoots, even a dusty speck
The first time spent it on a jolly trip
A vacation with mom, the camera I could skip
Little burnt, little sad, I waited for a month more
But the cherished times, healed my sore
The second time I enquired, joyful and glee
I had enough cash to be paid as fee
Then a sudden call came from a kin
A worry I could solve with the cash in my tin
Now, the third time, I have planned—all it takes,
On January 12th, an SLR would click my birthday cakes
Now, suddenly an opportunity has come for a tour
I might have a reason to travel to Singapore
Can I manage both, I was questioning myself?
Little math and a negative answer presented itself
Now I sit and wonder how ironic—this position
A place where I can click or, a camera in possession?
Why do you need an SLR, had questioned a friend?
Do you wish to be a photographer, follow the trend?
Oh what the hell, I photograph well even today
Would a point and shoot, make the image—ugly and grey?
So, I find my misery of months suddenly futile,
A desire I held dear, Oh so juvenile
I would rather travel, see the world with a naked eye
Capture it in memory, the beauty of the sky!

~Sam

P.S: True Story :)

Ashes—grey and dark

I stumbled into darkness;
Wandering in search of light
A boulder of grief; shattered my soul
Wings broke; before the flight

Where within me were hidden; these demons?
Where, when and how—they grew?
Why wasn't I aware of the wounds?
Beneath the skin—I am black and blue

Ache is now a blessed companion
It crumbles and strengthens my being
Yet within me are ashes; grey and dark
No reason for disagreeing!

~Sam

Monday, September 26, 2011

Survive some more

Beneath the smile,
Lays a wounded soul,
Scars many, a lasting pain,
One more blow, I couldn't care
Survived so far, will survive some more!

~Sam

Whirling leaf

I am a whirling leaf—with zest in my soul
As, lifeless, I float, to no where
Fallen from tree, into movement of wind
A granted blessing, of a humble prayer

Once clinging, living, feet tied to a bark
Bonding to every strand of life
Merry green and tender when born
Being bound to a place, my only strife

I swayed with the wind, I poured out my heart
Tell me what it feels—like, to fly?
In the end when I am a fallen leaf,
Would you hold me in your arms, when I die?

Take me to where, ever you go
Till I dry, crumble, touch the ground
Let the gust, tear me apart
But grant my wish, let me glide—unbound

~Sam

My whole world

What does my breath know?
Why I hold it when I see you
What does my time know?
Why it freezes when I think of you

What do my words know?
Why they can't express, what my eyes do
What do my ears know?
Why in your absence, they can hear you

What does your presence know?
Why it braces, my soul
What does your love know?
Why it defines, my whole world

~Sam

P.S: Am I in love? No. Do I have a crush? No.
Did someone break my heart? Nah. I am just gifted. ;)

Ignorant

How foolish was I, when I searched around
Seeking you in every one I met
How ignorant was I, all along
For you dwell in me, undiscovered as yet!

~Sam

Love-is in nature!

Love will spread open—like the endless sky
Brushed with crimson-pastel hues
One will grow wings, till, one can fly
Restrained no more—nothing to lose!

Love will fall like a withered leaf
In a silent life—dead, still, as a lake
A motion will set in a pleasant relief
For one is a lover—in wait, of the wake
Love will shimmer on everything—which, one is
Like the setting sun—that shines on the wide sea
Warmth, a cheer, will put one at ease
As long one can let—love be!

~Sam

P.S: I have been asked a million times about my inspiration for all the
love poems. Nature is one of the inspirations

Love Note (2)—Haiku!

Come along love, for-
I need company, bring with you-
Tune, a symphony!

~Sam

Like the wind [Haiku]

I am like the wind,
You sure, cannot, make me stay,
Till you breathe me in!

~Sam

P.S. It is a very simple haiku, little romantic and heartwarming
but if read between the lines there is more to it.

Wednesday, July 20, 2011

A Goodnight Wish . . .

Let not sleep bind my eyes
Until your memories adorn, the skies
Until your arms tuck, goodnights
Until your dreams bide, long after I arise

~Sam

Tuesday, June 28, 2011

Love Note (Haiku)

Tell me about love
That you wrapped around my heart
It grows everyday!

~Sam

Familiar Love

No violins played or flowers sprayed
No signals conveyed or conversations were made
But in a fleeting second—a feeling unexplained
Heart racing beneath the composure restrained

We were two smiling strangers in the drizzling rain
An unknown familiarity, but nothing to complain
Two steps backward a hesitant step forward
A wave of affection, a moment little awkward

A loving embrace, hearts entwined
Friendly greetings exchanged, identities defined
Is this the thing they called love?
What else can describe—we know each other how

-Sam

P.S: Nothing ;)

Heart of Gold

Lost in the merry and the cries of living
Burden of joy that didn't sprout from within
She embarked on a journey—to feel akin
To the beautiful soul that had been

She trotted the paths she had never known
She threw away everything she called her own
She trampled all once treated with glassy care
A realization of mundane—sordid satire

It wasn't the wisdom of the learned or the old
Nor it was the travel to a distance—far ashore
It was her spirit that unveiled a tale untold
A luminous smile-from her heart of gold!

~Sam

P.S. This poem is inspired by the main protagonist of the movie-
Eat Pray Love

A serenade..

Hope you too caught the beautiful moon
As lush clouds hugged the night sky

Hope with the breeze you felt attune
As music played when it brushed by

Hope you too danced slow somewhere far
As I cradled myself and gently swayed

Hope you too heard me sing alone
As it was for you—a serenade!

~Sam

Comedy Affair!!

It seemed like an endless endeavour
For this otherwise clever girl, however

She managed to confuse simple routes
Bought expensive plants without roots

She got wet in the rain in her office wear
She smiled at the ones with a shocked stare

Dropped money not a 100 but a grand on the road
Even managed to get her vehicle towed

She walked, she tripped, broke sandals on flat grounds
The laughter she spread was competitive to the clowns

The wind blew and messed up her hair
With ruffled bristles on head, she walked unaware

Didn't she worry, didn't she care?
With some flops everyday it was a comedy affair!!

~Sam

P.S. Based on the life of a real, living creature—me!

Parallel worlds

Our eyes glanced at the radiant sun
Dreams were dreamt on cotton clouds
Two pair of feet in synchrony, on the earth we ran
Days were spent dipped in the sherry
Conversations spun like forest fires
Hearts were numbed, unfazed in the rain

Mind unattended, begged to differ
Vision blinded under wraps of love
Million cells, once owned—lost self recognition
Mere responding to the rhythm of the paired
Thoughts suspended in a rut without care
World warned as days, months and years were done

Today we are here back to life
Eyes pinch, noticing the changes once uncared for
Time demands the years lived in a parallel world
People lost—blaming we ignored them all
The mirror faces an unknown image
Memories erased—what do we know?

~Sam

P.S: This. I think is a prose.

Nature Hearts..

When you pause to hear the iridescent rain
Your words sink but I drench in your thoughts

When you talk about the leaves, the swaying trees
Your images like the wind—tousle, brush past my mind

When you describe your lone walks in the Gulmohar lanes
I see a red hue blind my eyes and my heart blooms

When you tell me about nature, Like I tell it to the world
I know I have found you . . . a mate for my soul

~Sam

Let it go . . .

Dove, that flutters free in the sky
If I cage it won't its beauty die?

Flower, which adorns a youthful tree
If I cut it will its grace survive?

Wind, that blows, twirls and swirls
If I hold it in my arms can I make it stay?

Moon, that lights up the lovely night sky
If I clasp it in my palm won't the sight pale?

Love, wild, subtle and juvenile
If I lock it in my heart won't I stop it grow?

Life of worries, wishes and dreams . . .
If I could let it free, let it go!

~Sam

Wednesday, June 1, 2011

Gulmohar! (Haiku)

Glowing and fiery
In the mellow morning light
Eyes espied passion!

~Sam

Friday, May 20, 2011

Yawn! (Haiku)

Eyelids battle sleep
Flimsy night shadows the day
Stretched arms and a yawn!

~Sam

Thanks for the memories..

Thanks for the memories, I whisper into the air
Let it rove and halt, to find you somewhere
I see your blurred image, behind my shut eyes
A familiar stranger, I am caught in surprise
I've known you, I know—but I know not how
Let life unfold this mystery endowed
Thank you is all, I can hear myself say
For I find not better words-that can repay!

~Sam

P.S.: This poem is inspired by the novel—
"Thanks for the memories" by Cecelia Ahren

Few classic lines from the novel . . . "How close happiness and sadness are, so closely knitted together. Such a thin line, a thread-like divide that in the midst of emotions, it trembles blurring the territory of exact opposites. The movement is minute, like the thin thread of a spider's web that quivers under a raindrop."

Beautiful Enigma!

I waited long to find an answer
I met a gardener, a child and a dancer
Tell me what real beauty is, I asked
Teach me to see beyond the masked

The gardener walked me through the grass
Showed me a beauty none can surpass
Real beauty is like the miracle land
Unkempt mind tilled, with one's own hand

I asked the kid, what real beauty is
A pair of lips which on my wounded knee kiss
A hand that holds and wipes my tears
A heart I can open to and scare away my fears!

What is real beauty, I asked a dancer
Self-belief, self—pride was the simple answer
Real beauty is to feel at home in your skin
It is to feel the beauty, feel the dance within!

Real beauty to me, to you, is a different hue
But all our definitions are very true
For real beauty lies in each one of us
Beauty in different ways, we all posses!

~Sam

46

Autumn Maroon..

Hope flickers but dazzles like a clouded moon
Love slipped into deep slumber with no one to commune
But silken warmth still threads the heart like a cocoon
Waiting for a shade of the Autumn Maroon . . .

Like the roads that lay hidden, beneath the maple hue
Mundane days hide paths, that would lead to you
Though not a hint of direction or a dim clue
Faith wraps around my mind, and I pull through

I know, love is a wind one cannot chase
Like seasons of nature-with time it will embrace
Yet restlessness sets in, but no worry nor haste
A desire for search to meet the end, when our worlds interlace . . .

~Sam

Seeds of sorrow..

There was care in your recklessness
A sense of calmness in your restlessness
A sense of belonging in the myriad talks
A deeper meaning to the casual walks

You defined what it is to be ruled by the heart
You defined what it is to fall apart
You defined me as a woman I could never be
You defined a new me to me

When our paths cross, please pass a smile
Let my worries elude me for a while
For moments without you, like seeds of sorrow
Grow deeper into my heart with every tomorrow

Say a hello! Maybe once in a while
Let feelings for a second feel worthwhile
I know but I can't help—there is no other way
Cannot take back my heart after you swept it away!

~Sam

Caught in your rain!

Your words splatter, trickle down to my heart
Your sweet whispers splash, a colorful art!
I lie down without worry and kiss the falling rain
Celebrate this feeling with nature's champagne
I am flushed, I am rushed-I have no words to explain
Just soaking in your love while I am caught in your rain!

~Sam

Wednesday, May 4, 2011

Fragrance!

You bring with you my laughter
You fill my heart with Spring
Love blossoms each day
Onto your fragrance I cling!

~Sam

Changing Seasons..

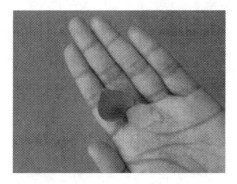

These leaves clasp the changing times
Like wind captured in the tune of chimes

The joy in the gait of a new season
Vivid change of colours, a worthy reason

The promising green and the celebrated yellow
Moments turning into memories mellow

Welcoming warmth and a teary depart
Goodbye kisses to mark a gleaming start!

~Sam

PS: A poem sang out of my heart when I clicked this picture.
Finally here it is—in words.

Snowflake!

A fragile crystal snowflake
Gently glides in the air
It makes me think about you
I hold my breath and stare!

Delicate pure serene love
That you sprinkle on my day
No less a miracle
Than this snowfall on my way

The sun rays that pat
And slowly melt the glaze
Remind me of your warmth
That set my heart ablaze!

~Sam

Speechless!

Look into my eyes
Read what I cannot tell
Enchanted by your love
I am cast under your spell

My heart grew a shade darker
It is deep crimson red
It slipped from my grip
Into your arms it fled!

You leave me speechless
No words, I just smile
I hush my heart to stay calm
Douse in you for a while!

~Sam

Love Note!

Your eyes give away what you hide
Your heart through your eyes confide
Conversing glances, words cannot define
I feel my heart dip in wine!

~Sam

P:S: I tried very hard to build this, add a line or two.
But these four lines—are complete. No addition was possible.

Morning delight!

I step onto the asphalt roads
As little crystals hug green leaves
The warm sun gently rises
A sacred morning it delicately weaves

Sunlight dances on the Gulmohar petals
As the road is carpeted with fallen flowers
A mild drizzle plays on my skin
As I am blissfully treated in these early hours!

A light whiff spreads in the air
As morning scent playfully sprays
Oh colours so vivid, a delight to eyes
Stunned by the beauty I mutely gaze!

~Sam

A recitation

Bliss locked up in its gentle fragrance
When earth dipped in rainy cologne
Each flower, each leaf adorned a diamond bead
Like lovers gift after a long adjourn

I step out and breathe a new air,
See the earth, still asleep like a new born
The rain in the dark, cast a mystic spell
To decipher it's symphony in the morn

The imprints on the ground
Trees pining for the rain that's long gone
Enchanted by recitation of a tale
In the drizzle at the break of the dawn!

~Sam

Life's Prelude!

A desire to push into the past, strongly brews
With merry memories, held as an excuse
To turn the hands of time, let worries elude
To re-live an age that is far ensued!

Make the mind twist to think like a child
Let it free; let it play for a while
To hold and behold dreams, dauntless
Unperturbed about the destined, mysterious

Be ignorant about the wrong and right
Without worry or fear let one's heart recite
To fall under a spell and momentarily delude
Trick a grown up to into the life's prelude!

~Sam

The flight!

I walk on the path afresh
To find foot prints of my folks
My heart swells with courage unknown
New responsibilities it evokes

Too grown up for one league
While young amongst the old
The wheel of life slowly creaks
In to a new role I mould

I shall try and do my supreme best
In to a new life I am reborn
Fly, live the dreams—yours and mine
With every blissful morn!

~Sam

Thursday, March 24, 2011

The Goddess

She sits clam amidst the gushing sea
Her breath a celestial symphony
The wind playing along her hair
Unleash supremacy unaware

The sea feels captive under a spell
As her dainty feet on its rock settle
Music glitters, sprays across the skies
As violin plays with her glancing eyes

When her hand glides over the sand
It quivers, ripples—loses command
The roaring waves caress her feet
Fall back mute and gently sweep

She rises like a pleasant cadence
Flowers bathe in her blissful fragrance
She is woman, a glory, a royalty
Mother Nature, a Goddess in harmony!

~Sam

Old man's strife!

I glance through my window
I see an old man
Walking across the lane
Coins juggling in his can

With every coin dropped
His eyes lit up
He wishes nothing great
Just a rice cup

I see him strain
Walking weak and thin
A kaput rough stick
His kith and kin

I caught his wise poignant eyes
Telling a tale of his tattered life
Once a young man's misfortunes
Now an old man's strife

~Sam

Answer my whys!

Mother O Mother
Can you answer my Whys?
I know no other
Who will answer me wise
You taught me to give little
From whatever I get
You taught me to cut into two
And share my bread

Then why I see, people cry?
One feasting over dinner
Sufficient for five?
While hungry people daily die?
Mother O Mother
Please answer me why
You told me I should never lie
Tell the truth when times try
Then why I see people blame?
Accusing each other
Making wrong claim?
Calling out a disgraceful name?
Mother O mother
Fight solves nothing is what you said
Anger is one's biggest threat
It does no good and causes regret
Then why do I see?
Nations engaging in war
Shameful world watching silently
The bloodshed galore?

Mother O mother
Didn't anyone teach them to be nice?
Or do we forget things once taught
And grow up to be unwise?

Mother O mother
Why doesn't the world know?
It baffles little kids like me
What I learn and what they show!

~Sam

Success!

I sweat I bleed,
I fight I proceed,
I fall I stand up,
I don't cry I hold up
I walk I run
With a goal I had begun
Finally I succeed
I am euphoric, I am freed!

~Sam

P.S: Success is underrated!

Free Spirit!

Like a bird in an open field
I, flutter away
Like water on a river
I hustle rustle and sway

Like the wind without destination
My heart gently glides
It ruffles few leaves on the way
But no where it resides

Nothing can root me to the ground
Nothing can make me stay
A free spirit I will remain
Come what may

~Sam

The confession!

I hear your words
The lovely things you say
Just how you say it
Is what makes my heart sway?

When I walk by your side
Having conversations undefined
Like a child on a swing
I freely unwind

I always wait
For your reassuring smile
It makes me feel beautiful
In my shabby old style

How casually you tuck
My hair behind the ear
I am too blinded now
Do I have to see clear?

Never thought I'd say these words
Or ever saw my feelings grow
I am madly in love
Now I let you know!

~Sam

For you, I pray!

Over thousand lives lost
Much more in pain
Empty broken houses
Roads red, with blood stain
Hues and cries
Dreadful screams
Watery hazy eyes
Over shattered dreams
Every heart froze
Eyes blinded with fear
Stable Earth toppled,
Like drunk, over a can of beer
How do they respond?
When lord pulled up the curtain
Suddenly staged a horrific play
Left actors with roles, uncertain?
All savings gone
Memories turned rubble
Oh dear nature
How could you cause this trouble?
My heart bleeds
As I hear people wail
Whom to hold responsible
Whom to put in a jail?
My only option now
Is to wipe a tear
And wish for recovery
In my daily prayer!

~Sam

End of the show!

Why do you still walk on my memory lane?
When I left you behind on a confused terrain
You had the company of a darling dame
I never loved you enough to be in the game!

Why does my mind splash the possibilities I have known
When I have already shut down this emotional cyclone
You are hopefully still merry and not alone
But my mind now battles a heart, overgrown

I am granted an unwanted wish, to be strong
I can feel no pain or no worry profound
My heart still intact, to luckier someone I shall bestow
I pull the curtains down, smile and sing its end of this show!

~Sam

Little heart!

My heart like a baby
Silently sleeps
It dreams of the pleasantries
Smile dimples its cheeks

Its two curious eyes
Too innocent but deep
It believes they will
Never have to weep

Its tiny two hands hold
Love so profound
It's grip too loose
With a faith unbound

It breaths slowly
Taking in life
One breath at a time
Its lungs fill it with goodness divine

With tiny steps
It walks on the ground
It will slip, it will trip
It can spin around

My heart like a baby
Doesn't care, doesn't know
It is still a little child
Which will someday, grow!

~Sam

How . . . ?

What did you whisper
To my cold heart?
You pierced through its walls
Like a shooting dart
Why does my mind
Decline to play its part?
Thoughts about you
Float like a fine art
What did you show
To my innocent eyes?
They have learned to read
What you convey in disguise
What did you do
To my lazy arms?
They embrace you close
Defying fear or alarms
How do you reach out to me
With your tender cajole?
And I let out to you
Feelings I withhold,
How did you teach me
To fall in love?
Gave my heart two wings
To flutter like a dove

~Sam

Beautiful Dawn!

Sometimes you might
Lose your belief
Life may seem just
Pain and grief
You might walk on roads
With a dead end
Or lose your way
Taking a wrong bend
You might be blinded
From your mission
And, all your actions
May, meet collision
Your logic might
Get you nowhere
And your faith might
Vanish in thin air
Life might have
A missing piece
And confusions might
Just increase
Whatever happens
Don't lose your belief
With a leap of faith
You will cross every reef
Never forget
Nature's simple norm
Dusk is always followed
By the beautiful dawn!

~Sam

Nature's Bond

Your presence
Like the winter breeze
Brushes my solitude
With a gentle tease
Your laughter like
The bright summer sun
Warms my soul
My dear one
My heart now plays
A melody tune
After you struck its walls
Like a typhoon
Something about the way
You hold my hand
All my worries
Just disband
Conversations we have
Simple, plain
Form clouds from which
Memories rain
By simple gestures
We correspond
Our love like
a nature's bond

~Sam

Ciao!

I packed my brain
Sent it on a memory drive
I relived few moments
And I felt alive
I shed a few tears
I won't lie
But the time has come
I have to say bye
I talked sense
To my bleeding heart
I made my friends promise
"We shall never part!"
Mentally preparing
Has worked I guess
My eyes now just
Look at progress
I am all set
For what's coming up next
I leave the ambiguity
Let my mind rest

I wave my hand
I take a bow
With a smile on my face
I am ready to go

~Sam

PS: This poem is especially dedicated to my batch mates and juniors
(from SDMIMD)

Temporary misguide

What is it that I like about you?
I can't seem to decide,
I don't feel much but
Have little something to hide

Just a careless conversation
Brings me back to the start
I laugh and brush it aside
As a joke of my confused heart

I know one thing for sure
It's just few things about you I like
And that it isn't good enough
To make the two of us strike

No harm in telling you
Oh I would take pride
But what good will it do?
It's a temporary misguide

~Sam

Anticipation

Wonder what it would be
When you'd find me and I'd find you
When we'd finally discover
A Love, that is true
If you too would like
The shimmering rain
Like to see it rustle,
Down, a window pane.
Would you too long
For affectionate smiles?
A hand to hold,
When you have to walk miles?
Would you need someone to cuddle
When lost, without clue?
Someone to talk
When you are down and blue?
Would your heart warm
To a particular tune?
Would you too feel romantic
When you watch the moon?
Would we laugh at jokes,
Only we would know?
Talk with our eyes
Watch each other grow?
We have never met each other
How would we know?
Whatever is in store for us
Only time shall show

~Sam

P.S: Happy Valentine's Day!! ♥

75

Surmise

My eyes lock on pretty dresses,
My skin demands some care.
I never bothered ever before,
But now I brush my hair!

My cupboard suddenly houses,
kurtas and a floral top.
My shoes are silently ignored,
My feet in dainty sandals hop.

A desire to look fine and nice,
No, it is not any of the guys.
I have no reason to tell lies,
No logical ground for this caprice.
Just the girl in me, I surmise.

~Sam

PS: Reality!

[Very soon . . . I will be banned for abusing use of PS!]

Write to me..

Don't call, just write to me
When you glance at the blue moon
That lights up the sky,
When you sit by a fire and watch
The ambers fly.
Don't call, just write to me
If you catch the sight,
Of a flower in bloom.
When you walk on a silent lane,
In the month of June.
Don't call, just write to me
When you connect to a soul,
You never knew.
Or made a kid smile,
Even for a moment or two.
Don't call, just write to me
When you do something,
You haven't done before.
Or you want to talk,
About someone you adore.
Don't call, just write to me
Not about your love,
Or what you feel for me.
But, about the man you are,
And who, you want to be.
Don't call, just write to me
Cause memories will fade,
But, words cannot tamper.
Don't call, just write to me,
Not about me, but, about you, on a paper.

~Sam

In simple words!

I can see you bowled over by me
But I like it that you do not show
I can feel your joy when I walk by your side
And I like it that you keep it low

At times I catch you stare
And you shake your head as I glare
I know you get lost in my eyes
But like it when you hide it with simple lies

The way you prefer to hug by a shoulder
Keeping it decent and not getting bolder
Simple ways in which you show some care
You give me my space but, tell me you are there

I can never express my affection
Or tell you how I appreciate this connection
All I can say is, my blood feels like wine
And I am really glad that you are mine.

~Sam

When you walk in the crowd,

And we steal glances.
At times catching myself laughing,
On the silly things you say.
I see what I feel for you.
Some attempts to show,
Your better side.
I pay stark attention,
Pick up little good things.
I see what I feel for you.
The days when my friends,
Laugh about your dumb jokes.
And I ruthlessly defend,
My illogical belief in your genius brain.
I see what I feel for you.
Those little moments when,
You stand somewhere close.
My ears picking up your every word,
Hearing you step away or near.
I see what I feel for you
My eyes trained to catch your image,
A silent hope that your's,
Would catch mine.
I see what I feel for you.
The way you are now a changed man,
More to yourself in a silent corner.

Your heart thrown away,
To that lucky someone.
The contented silly smile,
I see what I feel for you.
But that's just how crazy,
My sense will let me be.
Express a simple discomfort,
In a silly poem about how,
I see what I feel for you.

~Sam

PS: F.I.C.T.I.O.N (don't get too many ideas!)

Simple wishes

I want to douse in the sun on a chilly day,
I want to hug the clouds and lie down on the hay.
I want to trot on an unknown terrain,
I want to see the daisy caught in a window pane.

I want to root myself to the ground like a tree,
I want to flutter my wings and fly around like a bee.
I want to be warm like the summer sun,
I want to pour like rain, joy and fun.

I want to sing and hum like a cuckoo bird,
I want to match my steps with a sheep herd.
I want to touch a tree, let the wind tousle my hair.
I want to walk around free, show everything some care.

~Sam

PS: This was supposed to be a post.
But, this rhymes, so made into a poem.

Wednesday, October 2, 2013

The Writer's Date

In spite of the dullness and modest interiors of Oakwood, a quaint restaurant neatly tucked in the inner roads of Chenaati hill city; it had been patronized by creative artists, particularly writers who visited the hill station looking for peace and tranquillity required to write that yet another best seller. It was very common to spot one of these creative geniuses, downing numerous cups of coffee while looking dazedly outside the glass windows that were tainted to provide an apt level of privacy. One of the writers' who had frequented this place had described Oakwood to be that secluded nest amidst the laidback Chenaati, to where a creative mind could migrate to, if it were to drown in a slumber of undisturbed day dreams that artists usually need to engage in. If Oakwood was that secluded nest then, Paul, the waiter was its chirpiest cuckoo. Paul's verbose nature along with his satirical humour made him a man with a quality to be charming and irritating, both at the same time. Even his clean black suit with an audacious red bow tie, neatly trimmed handlebar moustache that curled at the ends, shiny boots and nose and well trained sophistication, didn't conceal that it's a very thin ice that needs to broken to make Paul speak his mind. A casual, "Can you suggest something nice to order?" could dangerously divert the conversation.

It was a usual slow weekday afternoon at the Oakwood with just one customer. The place was running on minimal staff due to the off-season. The tables missed the usual deal cards and the free bread trays that were served along with the salt, pepper, soy and Tabasco. A huge white board was displayed at the entrance trying to oversell a bunch of items that had been pre-cooked and were moving slow. A small bell hung at the entrance to announce the arrival of any customer to Paul and Deborah the only two waiters manning the restaurant. Deborah was to manage the odd numbered tables and Paul was to serve the customers occupying the even numbered tables.

Mr. Vincent, a regular visitor who lived across the street stormed out of the restaurant angrily, "For once, mind your business—you moron!"

Deborah lifted the Beer Mug with a cigar floating in it while clearing the table and shot at Paul, "Oh you must be proud. There goes my twenty bucks!"

Paul retorted, "Damn right, I am proud Deb! I did him a favour. He had no right to be rude to me."

"You just ordered a heart attack? How can you say something like that! Was that very polite? The man lost his brother a week back, because, of a Heart Attack! Didn't you hear the ambulance? You owe me my tip of twenty!" Deborah Said.

"Had I not said that? You would hear the ambulance, again and oh! Don't you worry about your twenty; I'll give you a forty. Go file your dirty nails, wax your hairy legs and flash them to your date." Paul shouted back.

"After what you said now, oh yes! You do owe me a forty." Deborah disappeared into the kitchen with the beer mug.

Paul dropped on his knees looking at the ceiling, "Oh Lord! I pray to you. Send in another customer before we kill each other."

The bell at the entrance chimed and the door swung open. A pair of Louboutins strapped to the feet of long legs peeking through a slit of an elegant floral gown walked in. A small white bag hung near the elbow of the lady's arm as she strutted into the restaurant like a life size Barbie. Her, Ken, Clovis followed her and gave a friendly smile as Paul stood up in a jiffy and greeted him, "Welcome Mr. Clovis! Didn't know you were in town. Writing another sequel, Sir?"

"It's all the mercy of the Lord! The usual table please." replied Clovis.

Paul bowed in acceptance and led the couple to a table by a window which looked onto a green park through the rain droplets that still lingered on the glass. Clovis checked with Claire, "Are you comfortable here, my dear?"

"Oh it's lovely darling!" She crossed her legs and freed her hand of the bag, resting it on the chair beside her.

Clovis took the chair that was diagonal to his date. He preferred to look at his women from a forty five degree angle. It gave him a satisfaction of being in a position to capture every little micro expression. After all he was a writer. There was nothing in his surrounding that wasn't a part of his notes.

Deborah pretended to be busy in the kitchen and hoped that Paul would request her for help in assisting the couple. The quarrel with Paul had killed her mood. She had a hot date in the evening and Paul's comment about her had just reminded her about how unattractive she looked.

Paul cleared the menu after taking the order and walked towards Deborah who ignored his presence, "Oh common! Are you angry at me now? Great!" Deborah didn't reply. She just turned her face away with a sudden spike in anger which occurs when one is confronted by the cause of the anger.

Much to her shock Paul walked straight to the writer's table, "Excuse me, Mr. Clovis; you are man of wise words. You have written so much about women that gives me the trust that you are a fairly enlightened man when it comes to the other gender. I have a problem here with my dear lady friend. May I have the pleasure of discussing this with you?" Paul turned around sincerely and requested Claire, "Of course with your permission Ma'am. Oh! And who better than a woman to know another woman, please feel free contribute to Sir's recommendations. Only if you don't mind"

Clovis looked at Claire and responded to Paul after a gentle nod from her, "Go ahead Paul. I have known you enough to consider you my friend. But know one thing; we are all amateurs when it comes to the other gender."

Paul took no time to ask his question, "So, if you were a friend of lady who is as ugly as a toad, is it fair of you to make a recommendation, which would make her look better?"

Clovis chuckled, "Not if you want to keep her as a friend. I wouldn't recommend that."

Paul looked Claire as if he waited for a response from her. But she gave none. He shot one glance towards the kitchen to catch Deborah watching them through the window screener. He continued, "Say supposing there was a glaring ugly mistake that your beautiful lady here made, wouldn't you correct her?"

Claire looked at Clovis as if this answer to this would determine the future of their dating. Clovis shifted in his chair and cleared his throat, "Hmmmm . . ." he breathed heavily before responding, "No!"

Claire raised her eyebrows and sharpened her gaze on Clovis. Paul quickly checked with her, "Is that something you would appreciate?"

Claire was quick to respond, "No. I'd like to be explained about something that I did wrong. I would value the honesty."

Clovis, "Value the honesty? I beg to differ, my dear. No woman has the stomach for honesty."

"That's because men are never completely honest with women. Why don't you be honest with me about something now? We can test the theory right here." Claire thumped her hand on the table.

Paul nodded in agreement. Clovis shifted uncomfortably in his chair, "I'll do that only if you give me immunity."

Claire replied, "Immunity for?"

Clovis bent forward and looked straight into her eyes, "Darling, I deeply admire and adore you. I definitely do not want this to blow it up for us. I need immunity that whatever I say next should never in the future or now be used by you as a reason to stop seeing me."

Claire was determined to make a point, moreover she was sure his observations would be trivial, "Oh give it try. You have the immunity!"

Clovis stood up, pulled out the chair beside Claire and stood behind her with his hand on her shoulders, "Here you go. Your breath smells of cabbage at times, and, at those times it is very hard to come near you. You legs are too long, and your Louboutins drill holes into my feet if I am not careful. Your house is like a pig sty which is ironical because you are so spic and span otherwise, like how you wipe your mouth every time you take a bite. Sometimes I just observe these little personality riddles, and it inspires me build fictitious characters. I do love these flaws"

Claire's eyes widened and her face turned deep red, "You love my flaws?" She picked her bag up and stormed towards the door and turned around, "Oh Paul! I stand corrected. Go apologise to your lady friend about your boorish, inconsiderate honestly and Mr. Clovis, please don't dare and come to my pig sty to convince me."

Clovis ran towards her, "Oh Claire! Dear, I told you no women, can stomach honesty." He held the door with his foot and watched his date walk away, "I'll call you in a week's time dear." Once she disappeared into the crowd he walked back into the restaurant and glared at Paul. Deborah rushed from the kitchen and walked towards Paul with her hands on her waist.

Paul stood there grinning, "You really didn't think I could pull that off did you?" Clovis broke into laughter and patted Paul's back, "With the confidence with which you accepted my proposal, I had no doubt you would! I've been trying so hard to break up with her. That gives me just that guilt free time and material I need to finish my story!" He pulled out a handsome amount of cash, pushed it in Paul's breast pocket and walked towards the door.

A shocked Deborah watched Paul count his cash.

"Thank you Mr. Clovis! May I know what your story is about?" asked Paul.

Clovis smiled, "Oh Paul! You won't be able to stomach the truth. Now go apologise to your lady." He pointed toward Deborah and walked out.

A year later Clovis released his third book which was a collection of short stories titled, "**20 Breakup Dishes**" centred on goofy waiters' whose conversations unknowingly lead to twenty couples breaking up. The thank you note read as follows,

"Thank you, my darling Claire for patiently accompanying me to twenty different restaurants, for enacting out the scenes from my imagination and giving me the opportunity to obtain live material from the oblivious waiters who played along beautifully.

Special thanks to the handpicked waiters who have always intrigued me with their personalities. This book is dedicated to you."

Friday, April 5, 2013

Coca-Cola

I run through the news channels impatiently to know the proceedings of a court case in relation to the verdict of a drug selling racket in India. It's been nine years since this case—this case that shook an entire nation and changed my whole life. The report that might be on the judge's desk right now has my name and a whole lot of papers that support my identity as a journalist assistant from Norway who has contributed significantly to the investigations. I could have been inside the court today waiting for a life imprisonment or crueller verdict—but no, I am here—sitting in my home in front of the television as a completely different person. Isn't that what I had asked for in return for my favour?

Over these years my hair has turned from black to grey. I am now a middle aged woman working with a government bank and my name is Agnes Brekke. I have two children, a husband and none of them know anything about my connection with the biggest Norwegian drug import to the Indian sub continent in the 1990s.

I had been to India with my then boyfriend in the February of 1991.I had befriended him through a university exercise on cultural journalism. He used to work with a magazine that published articles on various civilizations and life in different countries across different continents. Each student was assigned a journalist. And I had thanked my stars when I was assigned to the green eyed, unusually handsome man, Ethan. Ethan was in his mid thirties, usually dressed in his typical khakis and linen shirts. He had sported a beard that made him look intellectual. We continued seeing each other even long after I had graduated from my college and was interning with a local newspaper. Over my seventeen months of courtship with this man I never had a single moment of discomfort. Had the situation in India been little different I would have even sworn on my life that this man was innocent. I had really thought I knew everything about him. He had been travelling a lot around that time for different assignments in Africa, Canada and Cuba. So, when he mentioned that his magazine can sponsor an assistant for his new assignment in India—"Indian Fisherman-Their life at the borders" I jumped at the opportunity. I was to realize much later that this single decision was going to throw me spiraling down into the dark underworld of India and had it not been one opportune moment I would be there today in the Indian court listed as one of the accused facing potential life imprisonment in a foreign land.

"**Breaking news:** Ethan Aspen, the Norwegian journalist to serve life imprisonment over drug import and peddling charges in a nine year old case"

I am not sure if it is Ethan who is being walked out of the court into a police van. His face is covered with a bag. He looks much thinner, weaker and older. The news channel displays the quick facts about the case for the viewers.

Ethan Aspen—a Norwegian journalist assisted seven major drug imports into the Indian subcontinent.

The Nether dope was stuffed into waterproofed and gas filled barrels underneath cargo ships. These barrels would be dropped at a specific location by letting the gas out before the cargos reached the port. These barrels would then be picked up by an Indian fisherman who would coordinate the whole activity by a local drug peddler. Ethan interacted with these fishermen on the account of article coverage for a Norwegian Magazine and passed on critical information about the import. He communicated the Nether Dope sea hide spot destinations to random drug dealers operating through small unnoticeable retail kiosks only identifiable by a specific pattern of coca-cola advertisements painted in a coded fashion on their walls. The peddlers would in turn get in touch with the fishermen. Over 17 such outlets on Indian Highways were shutdown and the owners were prosecuted in connection with the most intelligent drug scandal. The information communicated was usually the nautical miles into the sea from the border and address of the fishermen who would assist in fishing out the Nether Dope barrels from the sea hide spots. He had aided three such imports from South Goa, Gokarna and Kovalam before the CBI was tipped off by an internal resource of the Norwegian Govt. Over 1500kgs of raw Nether—Dope was collected from various spots along the Indian Border during the course of the investigation. After long drawn political and underworld conspiracy Ethan is finally sentenced for life along with 13 other key accused.

After this summary they flash a photo of him at an outlet with coco cola painted on its walls. And highlight the coca-cola ads to display the pattern. I shiver because I was sitting right there about four feet away from Ethan when this shot was taken. I look at a photograph I had pulled out just hours ago. A photograph of me resting my head on a board painted with the coca-cola logo. A photograph that was the logical extension of the area photographed in the image that was being shown in the news. I light a cigarette to calm my nerves and continue to watch the news as the sweat drenches my t-shirt. I switch to multiple news channels covering the same news—they all show the same photograph, display the same pieces of information and like the first channel they too don't mention a Linda Schwartz in association with this case. The photograph on my table fails to appear in the news. I let out a sigh of relief and switch off the television. My body is still shaking with disbelief. I light one more cigarette and draw the smoke deep in till every inch of my lung is filled with it. I breathe the smoke out slowly realizing for the first time that my worst nightmare is over. I flip the photograph on my table. It reads

Name: Agnes Brekke
Norwegian Govt. Internal Resource ID: 8080NGZP
Cover: Linda Schwartz
Cover Profession: Assistant Journalist
Case ID: INDNDPO190383

My real identity had been made my cover and a new identity had been given to me.

The End

Thursday, March 7, 2013

Many Wines

She was sitting across the table with the prettiest face Eriq had ever seen. A beautiful black gown prided on her perfect body. But he could tell, she is not the kind that one could charm very easily. She looked at him with the eyes that demanded an interesting conversation. Eriq's reputation of being an Author usually set such expectations from the women he dated. What story could tell her, he wondered, rubbing his sharp chin.

"A story? Is that all I can offer to please you my lady?" He asked her in an attempt to buy more time.

"Aha . . . that is all. It's is not every day that one gets to share a drink with a writer." She looked straight into his eyes as if she challenged his art.

Eriq gazed at half empty wine bottle and pointed at it, "This . . . Reminds me of a story—a true story!" he said.

This was way back in the 1980's when I used to spend most of my holidays with Granny Medley. She lived in a town called Burfesco. It was a small commune nestled between the folds of two mountains. There was hardly any concrete there barring the cosy residential cottages with hipped roofs. That too, would be covered by green moss during the rainy season. This place was unheard of and was mostly uninhabited. Granny had her own versions about the history of the place. Some included the world war, something about the vineyards, but all versions were consistently hazy and conflicting. They usually depicted Grandpa as a Hero, were told over a glass of wine by a lady who was old and had a reputation of being tipsy.

It was generally known in the family that our beloved Granny who was once the smartest, the most widely travelled, the one that once personified elegance was now a funny old lady with partial amnesia and a flare for sharing stories from her past. May be that's what made it so easy to talk to her. There was nobody in the family who had not poured their heart out to Granny Medley. She would either have a remedy or a

90

story—either which way it would generally fix the issue. What more she couldn't help but forget the whole discussion. Of all the fixes that granny had provided in answer to my silly troubles of childhood and adolescence there is one thing which I remember very dearly. It was a pearl of wisdom rolled out by innocent Medley. I was completely unaware that I would carry it into my thirties as most simplified yardstick to ensure I was with the right woman.

It was the summer after my first serious girlfriend broke up with me. Anna, was a such a warm and affectionate girl. Mild, understanding and shy or so I thought about her. I had never imagined there would be a day when she would break up with me. She didn't even battle an eyelid while telling me it's over or that she found the relationship too listless! I watched her walk away wearing the bright orange half shoes and a white top little above where her jeans hugged her waist. Her golden hair bounced on her shoulders till she disappeared. Not once did she look back. And so I spoke about this to Medley in an attempt to understand this girl who changed her stand overnight.

"How old is she?" Medley asked as she read the labels of her priced wine collection in a teak cupboard.

"She's seventeen! Does that matter?" I snapped wondering if Medley actually heard my story or missed parts of it.

"Age is a factor, an important factor for a girl. Now, hold this bottle for me darling" she peered over her glasses giving me a reassuring look that some story or fix is coming my way. "Get two glasses dear, the round base ones placed in the second shelf from the right."

I reached out for the glasses and arranged them on the table next to the window overlooking Medley's little kitchen garden. "She didn't even look back Granny. What kind of girl does that? Aren't they supposed to be the emotional ones?"

She joined me near the table with another bottle and a cork screw. Her grey hair curled neatly below her ear. She has this posture she normally assumes when she talks about something serious. Her foot folds towards the side with her long skirt tucked behind her legs while she adjusted her glasses "Read out the year of the bottle next to you." She dismissed my questions.

"1982 White Merlot . . . This looks pinkish" I read out the italic words on the bottle that spoke about the greatness of French wines.

"This is the girl you dated. 1982 White Merlot!" she said after taking in a sip. "You know how it is made . . . ? The grape skin is left on to ferment for about four to five hours to give that hint of the grape tang. That pinkish hue . . . aha like first love! It gives you a fleeting feeling but when you grow older its taste is too immature for an experienced man or woman of tastes. Now sip this 1978, Merlot." She poured the wine just enough for a sip into the round based glass near me. "This is the girl who left you! 1978 . . . you will feel there is a whole new definition to the taste of Merlot. Unlike the 1982 . . . this one is very new in taste . . . the honey and cherry are sharper. Girls and young women are like freshly made wines that define the taste giving more definition to their lives and interests as they reach different milestones of their life. She left you probably because . . . you know . . . you were a Chardonnay . . . dry and different . . . . th" she stopped abruptly while looking outside window. "Oh dear, did I forget to pullout those carrots again!"

Anna, the girl I dearly loved is a bottle of Merlot and I was a Chardonnay? I let out a sigh of relief when Medley got up to take a look at the overgrown carrots. That was a conversation I didn't want to continue. But that was only until years later when I met more women and went through more and more heart break that I realized that Medley could have had a point. My first step after this realization was identifying the wine or the woman I wanted to be with.

Cabernet Sauvignon, they say is the queen of subtlety. Sauvignon has the strong flavour of dark fruits which is masked in its earthy taste. It is bold yet elegant with an essence that lingers after the drink is long finished.

Eriq, looked at the lady who seemed very pleased with the story. She would definitely find it romantic to be associated with a wine like Cabernet Sauvignon and then he threw in a question, "Which wine do you think you are?"

This had set the pace for the night and the writer had won his required audience. His Granny passed away when he was three. He had not gone through several heart breaks as he was usually the one to break up. Anna was nobody but an element of his fiction and Cabernet Sauvignon? That was the description he had read in the wine menu.

The End

**P.S: Writing after such a long break!
Wonder if it meets the expectations.**

Morning Dew

(C) Ashish Arora Photography

Dear Lorven,

I received your letter and I didn't know how to respond to it until today. Forgive me if I have made you feel forlorn or your love unrequited. But being a woman on the brink of love is like having a stormy wind inside the heart which rattles all the windows to oneself. She usually needs time to untangle and rationalize 'love' which she complicates in ways, which only she can understand.

As I walk here, through these fields, wearing pristine white, I feel as fresh and alive as the earth that has woken up to a warm sunshine. The day lures me with its splendid possibilities—tempting and teasing me to look at it with dreamy eyes, to wish, to hope, to fall in love and to have faith. My dear, you are like that golden hue I see in the sky—full of marvellous promises. I feel like a little bird getting ready for the first flight, I dream to spread my wings open and long to fade away into the bright sunshine you speak of. I wish to look at beauties of the diamond studded grass, the orange, the yellow, and the majestic landscapes with love brimming through my heart. And I long to escape to a different life, a life beyond the boundaries of self into togetherness and oneness—into a life where the horizon between the earth the sky fades, a life in which 'I' resonates to something more precious.

Yes, your love is ruling my heart right now. And, I am humbled by the majesty of this emotion. I am amazed at how the world is full of multiple layers. It's beauty unravelled by the depth of emotion with which one looks at it. My dear, I am looking at it right now under the magnifying glass of love and passion. I see a synchrony of lucid emotions that delicate, yet gracefully hold every breathing being as the world spins in fouettes. I am reborn into a new life with the supremacy of love. I feel like leaving everything behind right now to take a leap forward—to submit and to discover more. I have no fear, no concern nor a care of how it is all going to be. For my heart has commanded that I fall in love— deeply and truly.

—Ellie

Concealing Images

He sat in isolation looking at people around him. The sounds seemed to resonate in the air. He felt a tingling sensation on his back when music flooded through the speakers. His thoughts seemed interrupted as he touched the bridge of his nose in a futile attempt soften the pinch of unfamiliar glasses. Sipping the drink with caution he regained his focus. Every person who entered the bar was caught in his gaze. He looked at them with stark observation and shifted his eyes back to the next person who walked through the door. An unconscious disappointment emerged between slightly pressed lips every time he looked back at the entrance. As if, he tallied each person against a mental description of someone he seemed too eager to meet.

While he observed these people he seemed to know more about them than he wanted to know. Good people trying to be bad. People caught in the company of the bad. Peer pressure, social obligations all became visible to his eyes. He saw women, trading off their dignity to appear little fashionable and broadminded while their inner souls cringed with disgust, men gulping down more drinks than they can handle to reinforce their gender as if someone questioned them about it. Little scum bags killing time till they found someone who wouldn't be able to figure out a few missing notes from their heavy wallets. Bartenders entertaining guests they didn't care about. Everyone masked by concealing identities.

The tiny chips of mirrors on few of the walls transported him back to his school days when he was made to hold two mirrors in front of each other. He remembered the reflections, his astonishment when he looked in to the mirrors—Infinite images. His life seemed to be trapped in the illusion of these infinite images. A sadness wrapped around his heart when he recollected his ten year old self. He couldn't identify with himself anymore and yet he could connect to everybody around him. He had been through everything these people were facing and, a lot more. He felt his hands against his face as if to register how his visage looked like. He caught his image of in one of the reflections—a harmless young man dressed like it was his first visit to the place. The image disturbed him. He shut his eyes and rubbed the back of his neck in an attempt to let go of the emotions that seem to suffocate him. The metallic object tucked at his waist touched his skin and his lips pressed again—disappointment. But this time his eyes didn't have a shade of regret as if this disappointment was embedded to him and had become a part of his life.

He shifted the gaze to the entrance again and saw a group of girls walk in. Clam and composed he finished the drink observing each face. He followed the group as they walked and chatted with inexplicable joy and delight. Women—He sighed!

He focused his attention on one girl in particular. He battled the pity he felt for her. He saw her move to the dance floor. He didn't look at her directly. He caught her reflection behind his mirror image; a woman dressed in a colourful shirt and unusual green cotton trousers. Little stars hanging from delicate strings that were tied into a fashionable knot at her wrist. Beautiful flow of the curls, her hair swung around her as she danced to an incomprehensible beat. He gave an unconscious nod as if reassuring himself of something. In the next few minutes the reflection of the women fell on the floor with blood splattered across her face. The mirrors held reflections of people horrified by what had happened.

He? He disappeared into one of the infinite concealing images. The gun felt hot tucked at his waist. Lips pressed with disappointment but his eyes—no regret. His way of dealing with guilt was putting the blame on the people who hired him. As long as there was someone wanting someone else dead—it could be anyone who could become the killer. This day, this time, this life—it was him.

Lift Man

"Here you go" he handed the badge with a stinging stare literally thrusting it into my palm. If I made any noise it wasn't heard. He was too tired of doing this for me and he made no effort to conceal the obvious irritation. "You know how hard it is to get you a job?" his eyes flamed, more out of concern than anger. I just nodded in response. He kicked his dhoti in a swift movement and grabbed it by his right hand. With a despairing expression he disappeared into the crowd. I wondered how much he loved his sister and my mother that he puts up with this trouble of finding me a job again and again.

I waited for the door to open and stepped into a 3x3 space marked by a transparent cabin overlooking the interiors of a fancy building. That defined the boundaries of my work area. A panel of nine push buttons greeted me. The building had six floors. There was a button for each floor. Two buttons to control the closing and opening of the door and one emergency stop. I had a brief training session in the morning. A huge man in security uniform instructed with stern voice pointing a stick at an LED board, "This will glow when the number of people in the lift is more than what it can handle. Ten people, and not fat ones like me" he tapped on his bloated belly. This followed with few other emergency precautions and protocols, attendance register entry instructions, salary deposits and building rules for support staff.

Given my condition, moving up and down in a lift full off people day in and day out, was not what I had dreamt of. Anyhow, I was worried about keeping my job. Ramu mamu had given his word to the owner. I couldn't let him down. I sat on the stool placed near the right corner. I lifted my hand and tried to touch the farthest button. I could sit and still access it. Phew! As the clock struck 10:00am people started flowing in and out of the building. It was a shopping complex—books, music, apparel and what not. I panicked worrying should there be an awkward moment where I could get stuck. But the day passed by pushing buttons—1st floor, 2nd . . . . 4th again and again. While some mentioned the floor some just took names of the shops and I had to refer the small chart given by the security guy to figure out which floor they had to get to.

It was very strange how minimum people spoke. May be that was how they became in the crowd—mute. There was this pregnant lady wondering about getting into a crowded lift and her husband grabbed her shoulder in an assuring manner while signalling me they will wait for the next round. No words spoken. Similar conversation occurred when an over energetic little kid pestered his dad to take the lift. I smiled as the wide eyed kid repeated "Wow" innumerable number of times, fascinated with the movement of the lift. He made me feel like I had the coolest job in the world. His dad made a futile attempt to cover his embarrassment with a smile. On countless occasions, I held the door open and waited a bit longer when I saw people rushing towards the lift door. I helped people when they struggled with handful of bags. They spoke to me with their expressions and emotions that rang out loud even when they restrained their voices. And, I, just felt normal. There was no chance they would know. And, no reason for it to be explicitly told, the job was getting done and communication was effective.

That evening when Ramu mamu came to pick to me up my lips moved to thank the man for my new job. A job—that made a voiceless man, feel normal and vocal.

Monday, May 28, 2012

The Old Charm

As she locked the main gate and walked towards her house she took a moment to look at the neon lights that painted the air orange. A wooden step ladder silently slept against the wall. She had used it to change the fuse. She decided she would push it to the store room the following morning. She looked at the brightly decorated door and its thick green border with a deep sense of satisfaction. She had insisted she work on it herself rather than getting it done by someone else—it was her house after all. Though this looked a tad too bright she was happy that it spoke of her creativity which she had tucked deep inside her after her childhood days. Little reluctant to push the door open she sat on the stairs and looked into the blank night.

Her mind kept drifting from one thing to another even though everything was taken care of. The stock for the opening day was procured, the chefs were summoned to report by seven in the morning, the lights were up, plants neatly decorated and she had also carefully ironed a sober pink and beige saree for the D—Day. Did I? She wondered about arrangement of the new addition of tables in what was her living room until today. She wondered how it would feel, this shift from securing herself behind locked doors each day to opening them for complete strangers for the days to come. A home restaurant, is that what they call these houses converted to serve food? If yes, that that was what her home would be transformed into, starting tomorrow. She didn't think of any name for commercializing the place. Giving a restaurant name to her house didn't go well with her. Anyway it was a small neighbourhood. The word would spread with the help of friends and loved ones and it would be fine.

She felt the breeze brush against her face and she untied her hair. The wind played with her grey strand and she let out a sigh of relief. The part of saree which hung from her shoulder floated in the air and she tucked the mischievous end into her waist in a well practiced swift movement.

She shut her eyes to cease the moment and questioned herself about what everyone else had questioned her about, "Why suddenly? Why at this age?" She felt her face and straightened the folds on her skin—how old did she look anyway and what had age got to do with a dream? A simple dream, and if not now then when? These questions had haunted her for a while. She had always wanted to do something but it was always the parents/in-laws, the husband or the kids. Now that she was free from all responsibilities she felt like a twenty year old waiting with anticipation about the possibilities of how life would unfold. The investment was very little so it was a calculated risk. She had retained the home interiors as was and added a couple of more sofa sets and tables. She unloaded an old carton, full of extra utensils which were carefully stored after her children moved out for starting on with their own lives. It was just she and her husband from thereon until two years ago when an unexpected heart attack left changed the situation. Does age make it easier to deal with grief or it was just she who handled remorse along with a hope to utilize a new lease of freedom? A tear trickled down her cheek and she wiped it off before the guilt or pain could weaken her. She had to prepare for tomorrow. She pulled out a crumbled piece of paper and read out the menu she had planned for.

Eight years later her children inherited a profit making home restaurant in the suburbs of Delhi that had become famous by the name of The Old Charm. It was an affectionate name that came into being out of love and respect for the seventy five year old entrepreneur.

The End

Rusted Memorabilia

I have a small motorcycle shop next to a bus stand. I was living my dream when I invested my humble savings of eight years at a factory to raise that three walled structure with a white metallic door. I remember leaving no effort unturned to make it look like a decent repair shop for a man who rode a proud Enfield or a Karizma to stop and get the bike repaired. In first year of the shop I cribbed, cried and wiped the careless grease or oil that landed on my floor or on my white door. My hard earned money. This place justified my eight year slog and the first year of business which was now slowly reaping thin but steady profits. Spotless it should be.

All this meaningless cleaning became a complete waste the day I saw a heart scraped out of the white coating of my garage door. As if mocking my disdain the culprit had written his and his beloved's name along with the date—16/10/05.

I was grumpy the whole day and following morning I forced myself out of bed to walk and open that distasteful door. "You are too prim and proper for a garage man" my customer poked his nose into my issue. "If I left the grease unclean on your bike how would it feel?" I responded without looking up and continued to fix the carburettor. His hand rested on my back with a pat of pity. "Arreh, seems like you never proclaimed your love Arshad Bhai! Let them write their hopes and scribble their names your door. Roshan loves Divya! Aha! Beautiful Arshad Bhai, beautiful! I mean good thing nobody scribbled that F word or some lame thing on your door."

At that moment I was too hurt to know something worse could have happened. But as if my customer's tongue marked its way onto my door the next day I saw an incomprehensible word scribbled along with few more hearts and love declarations. I painted that part of the door but in vain, here came the rains and the words peeped through with a rusty finish. But over the past five years with seven more additional labours and another garage space I had little time to be bothered by these scribbling. In fact I had converted it as storage for spare parts and it remained shut most of the time.

It had finally planned to get rid of the door and replace it with new one. A fresh white metallic sheet with its hinges fastened leaned on the wall as it was scheduled to be fit the next day. That day morning as I sipped tea monitoring the fitting and cleaning of couple of bikes a lanky young chap came by. "What?" I asked almost annoyed by the incomprehensible expression on his face. Hesitatingly with a sheepish smile he enquired about the old garage with a white door. "Arshad motorcycles, yes, there was a small garage na uncle?" Worried about the recent government poaching of the land areas I stood firm of feet and replied pointing towards the structure, "That belongs to me. Why?" He followed the direction, quickly took snap and walked by, "Five years since I first scribbled our names on this door. Tomorrow I get married to her. This photo will be a sweet memory of how it all began!"

Before I could gather what happed he muttered a polite thanks and walked away. "Arreh, bhai! What's your name?" I shouted in an attempt to know at least one of the culprits. "Roshan and Divya" he smiled like a little boy when he said that. I stood there and stared the priceless marvel of the rascal whom I scorned day and night for many months. I broke out into a smile and decided to leave the door standing for few more days—a journal to bring alive the rusted memories of loving souls.

The End

Deewana Dewaar Karigar

The air was still. The floor polishers, hammers, saws and drills that groaned throughout the day rested silently like tired young children who have played longer than what they could endure. The wooden support structure that served the purpose of enabling movement up and down the partially constructed building creaked as he bent forward. About three storeys high, he inclined at an impossible angle. Achieving it by resting his hands alternatively on the wall each time he scraped out the extra cement on the wall. His eye squinted in the flickering light to observe the protruding portions of the wall. His hand followed his vision and he gave a confirmative nod as his fingers felt the asymmetry of the surface. With a tiny metal piece that was strapped with sand paper on either side he started his chore. He blew away the chipped off excess cement in a practiced manner after every screeching stoke he made on the wall. His black hair was grey with dust.

Here was a man, a perfectionist, an artist of his own kind—a *Dewaar Karigar*. Slight buzz of *desi daaru*, gentle breeze that made his skin feel soft like that of a child, the day mellowed down by the night and only a dash of yellow street lamp to add to the moonlight—that was when he worked his magic. He would be summoned only for the luxurious buildings that demanded stark perfection. With the credit of smoothing the walls of great museums to MLA houses to perfection he was the man who needed no introduction. He was often referred as *Deewana Dewaar Karigar, Museum Wala*. With the exception of long lost family and childhood friends nobody knew his real name. He too preferred to be called—*Deewana*. His name *Amit* flooded him with memories of his mother calling out to him on the crowded street. He preferred not to be reminded of the past. *Deewana* was what he had become. And, the identity of *Deewana Dewaar Karigar* was his source of livelihood.

It was only in the moments of solitude like this, when his hand monotonously preformed the act while his mind eased under the influence of little alcohol that he strayed into the streets of the past. Of a beautiful childhood, a social discord, a journey of discovering an art and, the evolving of an orphaned *Amit* into *Deewana*.

"Arreh, spread it nicely. It should be smooth!" Kattu Kaka and his clicking of the tongue, "Tch tch tch . . . Smooth Smooth . . ." he used to lift Amit's hand and rub it against the wall. "Feel the flatness of the surface! Smooth . . . Smooth. Get it?" He never liked Kattu Kaka as a kid but now he smiled whenever he thought about him. He had met him on one of the construction sites. He was struggling to pick up the bricks with his barely ten year old tender hands when Kattu Kaka had called out to him, "Oye Bacche! Come here . . . leave those bricks and help me with this." He had instructed him squat on the floor next to cement mix poured into a pail and handed him a flat piece of metal with a handle. It was that 2 feet patch from the floor that Kattu Kaka found difficult to work on. Amit's small frame could manage it with ease. Kaka squatted next to him and showed him basic movements to flatten the surface of a newly built wall. It was on one such occasion that Amit had discovered the beauty of the chore.

The repeated reprimands and an occasional slap at the back of his head made Kattu Kaka a monster in his premature mind. When he was about twelve he fled to Kolkatta with a group of construction men he had befriended. Over the years he met many *Dewaar Karigars* in different places with different styles and approaches to the task but the artistry behind that job was Kattu Kaka's gift to him. However he appreciated the man he never thought of going back to him. He was by himself now.

On the majestic smooth wall of a glorious building that gleamed under the golden rays of the sun nobody noticed the faint print of a kiss—an artist's token of admiration of his own art. When the morning dew settled on the wooden structure and traces of day appeared on the still dark sky, *Deewana Dewaar Karigar* slipped his tools into the back of his trouser and silently disappeared with a couple of hundred that would nourish him with the required food and make him dizzy with some alcohol. His price wasn't the money it was that momentary escape into the life that was numbed by reality and that pride of having delivered a perfect art.

Tuesday, February 7, 2012

A Momentary Distraction

Life seemed to be stuck in a monotonous rut. Not that I had any complains about it but I wasn't particularly happy either. I had a steady income, a wife who had adjusted to my life so well that I had the luxury to overlook my own children, not because I didn't care for them but because I knew she could manage. I was walking towards my car after a regular day at work when I saw an ugly dent on the right edge of the bonnet. I had the insurance. I was calm but the thought that somebody wrecked my car and walked away free left me with an unsettled feeling. When I came a bit closer I saw a piece of paper flutter with it one edge clipped under the wiper. It read, "Sorry, a careless mistake. Was in a hurry so couldn't wait. Call 98734-87632 an incomprehensible name was scribbled on the same paper, R . . . Re . . . Rev . . . Argh some name. I tucked in the pocket and went straight to the garage to get it fixed. When the bill came up to 8k I decided to give the person a call.

What did I expect—A rough coarse voice of man, reckless, careless, picking the call only at the nth minute when the ring was about to die out. "Hello" A chirpy voice of who seemed like a charming lady spoke at the end other. A smile instantly crept on my lips. Not that I didn't love my wife but it was the excitement of the unexpected tryst with an unfamiliar woman not initiated by myself but by chance. I glanced at the bill in my hand partly absent minded and partly unsure of my words. "I got your number on my dented car. Some hurry you were in!" She let out a big "Oh!" almost like that bit was erased from her memory and this sudden reminder had saddened her. "I am soooooo sorry!" How typical! Isn't that what every woman says? As amusing as it was I wasn't ready to let go of the 8k bill her sorry had caused, "Could you please let me know how I am going to be reimbursed for the damage caused?" I put it out right there like a jackass. I didn't want to be gentleman; I didn't want to be the good guy. I had no need to. I didn't have to impress anybody.

"Yes . . . yes . . . That is exactly why I left my number. Oh I am Raksha by the way. And you are?"

I was waiting at the entrance of a fifteen storied structure some, Royal Arcade. When she came it was very easy to spot her. She was in hurry, almost like her feet moved at a fast pace mindlessly. Her neck was bent towards the right and her mobile locked safe between the grip of her shoulder and the tilted head. I was ready to let go of the initial impression of a dumb woman oh was she charming or what! She gave a sheepish smile when I waved my hand at her and pulled out the cash in an elegantly wrapped paper. Her transparent features played regret when she said, "I am sorry! I am soo sooo sorry!" Before I could think any better I heard myself speak, "Don't bother. I have insurance. I just wanted to see who caused the damage. I am not disappointed I must say. A cup of coffee?"

It never occurred to me the thought of wife, the mother of my children. I flirted like a college boy, amused by every silly thing she did. Just, when, we were about part and say our goodbyes I suggested the next meet, "You are an interesting woman. You should definitely meet my wife. You both should get along very well. Do come by sometime." Her eyebrows furrowed almost instantly and I walked away with smile. A momentary distraction and nothing more is what a man needs.

The End

Midnight Ballet

The room was elegant. It displayed a profound association with artistic taste. The antique furniture, huge photographs of a ballet dancer framed in creative wooden bends, the shade of mystic orange adorning the walls and the royal cutlery charmingly peeking from cupboards of various sizes were the proof. The fragile old woman who catches wisps of sleep on a metallic chair looks out of place—a misfit in her own house, a jarring present of a glorious past.

It is only when the tuned television blares into a merry ballet song that she opens her eyes, puckering her lips into a smile. Though her old self is a stark contrast to the woman in the photographs there is no doubt about the dancer she had been when her face beams as she rubs her eyes to catch the ballet on the television. She lifts her delicate arms and swings them to the music with perfection like they were given to her just to be able to do that. A melodious hum matches her little dance and she swivels her wheel chair in sync with the rhythm. A joy fills her heart, elates her feet gives them the life they do not have. The sorrows of an unfortunate event that cut short her majestic career suddenly and a lonely life that followed her into the old age are too insignificant, too unworthy of this one hour of her day. Her eyes remain closed but she sees a stage.

This is that one hour that she dances her way into the past, not with her body but her soul. It is divine to feel no limitation, no boundary to the joy. To feel detached from the existence of an earthly being and rising to be a dancer who paints emotions with the twists and twirls, rhythm and beats. The remaining hours of the day were like that waiting before an on stage performance. Her heart looking forward for the clock to strike eleven, her ears anticipating the music they would play today and the audience were her belongings in the house which gathered dust only to be shaken to the vibrations of a song. It was all she lived for—that performance in her own midnight ballet.

It was not a match to the performances she had given in the past but the world it transported her into—that was the best appreciation she had ever received. Someday she would silently close her eyes never to open them again to get transported into that world of ballet forever and make a grand entrance to—another stage?

Gift of Gratitude

She woke up from the sleep by a rude disturbance, "Quick, you don't have time!" her mother screamed into her ears which shook her awake. She rubbed the sleep from her eyes and walked nimbly to the courtyard. While she splashed water and cleaned—a basket full of jasmines waited for her patiently. In a swift movement she picked it up and headed to the Temple. "Mala, don't stay out too long. Come back for lunch!" her mother instructed with concern.

Mala, was a girl of ten. She had grown up seeing her dad come home with a huge sack for fresh flowers. Her parents would then carpet the floor with jute bags and splash water over it. She would sit still and watch as they continued this chore religiously each day. The flowers would be spread on the wet jute sacks. Her dad would chop off the green stalks while her mother meticulously strung the colourful flowers together in beautiful garlands. Different scents signified different seasons. But there was one constant the—Jasmine, her mother had explained was a fragrant emblem of gratitude to the lord, the princess of flowers. And, it was bought all round the year hence forming a source for steady income into their family.

In the initial years had mother had tagged her along because she didn't want to leave the child alone but the girl grew to become and more interested in the profession, till she decided she should manage to sell a basket of Jasmines all by herself. So this was one of those early morning when she would walk to the nearby temple, offer the best flower in the basket to the Lord and carry on with the selling to return back only when basket was empty.

She walked from one street to another, identifying people who were likely to buy a garland of flowers it was then that she saw this woman, a thirty something lady, frantically searching for something from her purse. Mala waited till the lady's mission was accomplished and then took a step towards her bright blue car, flowers hung from her printed cotton bag as she stretched her little arm and propped it on the car window, "Just Rs.10 per garland" The lady's face softened with the scent of fresh jasmine. She smiled and cheerfully paid for a garland. When Mala was about to walk back, then the lady called out to her softly, "Hey! Thank you"

Mala didn't know what it meant. She thought about that pleasant expression on that woman's face. A warm and beaming smile as she spoke those two words—"Thank you. Thank you. Thank you." Mala repeated it trying to smile as she lay on her bed before the final moments of sleep dawned upon her. The next day she asked her friend Appu, "Do they teach—Thank you in your night school?" Her little companion jumped with glee," They do! They do! It means—Thanks-gratitude" before she could ask anything else Appu disappeared into the market to continue her selling. Mala sat at the exact location as yesterday wishing she would see the lady again. While she waited, "Thank you Thank you." She practiced the expression till she got it correct. It moved her deeply to be able to say those two words.

The following day when her mother woke her up she uttered the magical words, "Thank you. Thank you Amma." The baffled expression of her mom eased when she saw Mala smile. "I am grateful." Her mother smiled and carried on with the day. Mala did the same things she did everyday but today each interaction ended with "Thank you." When people bought garlands from her she smiled beaming, expressing her gratitude—"Thank you." She managed to empty the basket much earlier than ever and there was this immense peace, a little joy when she saw people smile as she said those miraculous words. It was in the late evening, when she saw the lady in the blue car, before she could reach her, the car had moved keeping pace with the change in the traffic signal. Mala held the last garland of Jasmines; she had kept aside just in case she saw the lady in the blue car again. A fragrant emblem of gratitude, coupled with two words from the depth of her heart which she murmured to the lady who faded into the crowd,—"*Thank you!*" And a smile bent her lips and lightened her heart.

The End

Unknown Beloved

I saw *her* for the first time on one of the busiest streets. How gracefully she hopped from the pavement onto the road and stretched her hand instructing the vehicles to slow down as she crossed the path. Just that faint recollection of her crossing the motorway lingered on my memory like the scent of a lovely perfume. How much ever I wished to see her, our paths refused to meet until the day I spotted her walking into a jewellery shop. I made no mistake in recognizing her. I couldn't. Before I could think better my feet were racing towards her and I found myself helplessly glancing at a very vast space with innumerable counters. When I swivelled to complete a full sweep of the place with my eyes, I caught her walk out of the building. This time I pulled myself together. I was a respectable man. This was unlike me; I knew I shouldn't be chasing her. However, I did spend the following few weeks regretting how I lost an opportunity to probably get to know her.

As the months passed she slipped from my thoughts. But, I found myself filled with the same cheer when I spotted her on a random official occasion. Our tables were diagonally placed. I strained my neck each time to catch a glimpse of the woman who was unmistakeably her. As the occasion neared the closing time, I buttoned my coat and walked to her extending my hand introducing myself, "Hello lady! How delighted I am to see you here today. I have known you since the past couple of years and have been waiting to be introduced to you. But, I was never able to get to know who you are. Pardon me for introducing myself to you this way. But I have been enamoured by you each time my life was graced by your presence in the same surroundings. I am a respectable man; I work with the Stocks. I would be delighted if we could exchange words over dinner." Her eyebrows furrowed and she appeared unsure, "I am so sorry; I am really humbled by this encounter. But, I do not extend my company to men I do not know." I quickly found my business card and handed it to her, "Here are all the details of the man dear lady. Pardon the foolishness of the person I have become after being caught in this tame-less passionate yearning."

She signalled me to take a seat in the table for four where she sat unaccompanied. It was utmost pleasurable to finally be at a discreet distance from her, to look at her features, the colour of eyes, the fall of her locks and the smile on her lips. I gathered myself and initiated the conversation by talking about my family, where I was from and asked more about her. By the time the food arrived, I regretted my folly for having unabashedly expressed my desire for a woman I know nothing about. Each time there was a stance to be taken on a topic or a perception to be presented in the context of the conversation, we both invariably took different stands. We engaged ourselves by covering the awkward silences by inappropriate laughter or unnecessary feeding of ourselves in an attempt to buy time to think of more words. When the dinner ended, I bid the lady goodbye and we both exchanged courtesies of calling back. She was charming yet intelligent, graceful and humble. But, the additional attributes added to that faint sketch of a woman I have envisioned based on my frivolous encounters with her over the two year—I was disappointed. I even dreaded receiving a call, though it was apparent she would never make use of the card to contact me nor I would make an attempt to get in touch with her.

It was a year later that I saw her again. I considered exchanging a smile, because of the inescapable familiarity that showed on both our faces. But then she looked straight ahead and disappeared into the crowd. I gasped a sigh of relief. It is strange, this—zealous longing. How silly that we build a person from fragments of our imagination. And sometimes we do it so well that we develop this affection for an unreal person/fancy which may be very different from the real being who enticed us into this desire to begin with. I turn my head to catch a glimpse of her and she crosses the street in the same manner she did years ago. The faint image of the lady—there she is—*a unknown beloved*. And knowing her—changed it all.

The End

A Christmas Hug

The weather was cold and breezy. I pushed opened the stubborn door jammed with ice crystals. The air swished through the three layers of drapes and left a trail of goose bumps on my skin. There was festivity in the air. The rustle of leaves chimed with the fading sounds of giggles and carol which reached my ears.

My mind was preoccupied with thoughts. The taste of the passing year lingered on my being. It had been a year of parting, a year I wished I had never witnessed, a year of the loss of a beloved. If it had not been for that unfortunate day I would be smoking my pipe reading the Christmas offers to her, breathing in the heavenly smell of home baked cake and my ears would have been tuning to the hum of *twelve days of Christmas* that never left her lips even long after festival. My eyes feel misty, my heart warms and I hum for her.

I cross the houses which are beautifully decorated, the colourful lights glistening on the snow. She would clap her hands with glee when she saw something so beautiful. Reminds me of those long Christmas strolls— we were like children at sixty, joining people in the songs, looking at snowmen and sitting at the park bench with our hands interlaced like a young boy and girl, their hearts still excited about the first love.

I can't walk anymore. The memories tire me. My feet refuse to move. Tears threaten to roll down my cheeks when I look at the bench where we used to sit. How did I reach here? My feet just moved, and there was no other place I wanted to be. No other place where I could imagine her to be. I sit on the bench alone and look up at the sky. The stars shine beautifully. It feels like a thousand angels are assuring me, whispering to me that my love is being taken care of. I see her smiling face. I blow a kiss into the sky. I pull out the silken pink print scarf, she always wrapped around her neck—she was such a charm. I place it on the bench, with a small card attached to it.

I lower my head and walk back slowly, the burden of parting weaning my strength. "Hey!" someone calls out. It cannot be for me. I keep walking, dragging my feet slowly. "Hey! Wait up!" I turn around—the intrusion of a private moment annoys me. "What!" I scream back only to regret it after I see a little girl. She looks like a tiny woollen ball in all those winter clothes. Her face red with the winter rash, she waits till my face softens and the annoyance mellows down, "I am giving Christmas hugs." The big smile on her face is infectious. I wrap my arms around the little child standing with her hands stretched. I hug her as tears wet my eyes, "Merry Christmas Dear" I wish her with all my heart. She plants an affectionate kiss on my cheeks and runs away for her next hug.

I stand there in awe, the warmth still comforting my body. The little girl's love still blushes my cheek. My soul feels liberated. I look up towards the sky and express my thanks for the gift—A Christmas Hug.

P.S: Merry Christmas!!

Friday, December 16, 2011

A Timeless Bond

(c) Ashish Arora Photography

It is very difficult to have your entire life changed by one moment in which a man ties a yellow thread around your neck and the world proclaims you as his wife. And, that is the moment when it all begins—the change begins.

I have moved to a city I had never been to, I was living with a man I didn't know, I was wearing the uncomfortable sarees, a vermillion mark had suddenly defined, how, where and with whom I should live. I blamed all the change on him for while but still dutifully tried to fit into his life through the little gaps, every man has. A steaming cup of coffee, just as he woke up was his greatest delight. It pleasured me to see him happy and yet there was some disconnect. It wasn't him, it was the newness. Four months had passed, but that newness still lingered in all our interactions. We slept without facing each other, ate without speaking, and walked as though there was an invisible person who walked in between us. He would be careful not to make me uncomfortable and I would make sure, I conveyed, how much it meant. If not love, there was mutual care and understanding.

There were days when I spent hours trying to settle my feelings towards this man I was slowly feeling attached to. I had realized that sublime desire to belong to him, to become an inseparable part of life, beyond his dependence on me for the daily errands. To look at him as a husband, rather than someone my destiny was entwined to, to feel, the pride to walk by his side, to look at his eyes for reassurance, to feel that desire for him. I liked his presence in the house. That faint smell of castor oil he applied to his hair or the way he watched the news and grumbled when it didn't please him. But, there was something that held me back.

When we found words to interact with each other he had bluntly asked pinching his nose, "You like Jasmines? I find the scent of that flower a little suffocating." I told him they reminded me of home and he smiled as if didn't bother him any longer. Though little unsure, I asked something that had been nagging for a while, "Why do you wear those white shirts, starched and stiff? It gives me a feeling I live with a politician." He laughed as he spoke, "They remind me of my Dad. He was a parliament member" I smiled. It didn't feel that odd now.

The following day, as soon as he left for office—I pulled out a five hundred, from the money my parents had given me when I left home. I went to the shop which was just round the corner and bought him a shirt—white like he liked, but with a little design the way, I liked. I struggled through the afternoon waiting for him to get back. And yet, when he was home I hid the shirt away and disappeared into the kitchen. What will I tell him? How will I give it to him? Would he like the shirt? Would he wear it?

He went to the room to freshen up and I was placing the food on the table when the familiar scent of Jasmine filled the room. I notice a bunch of Jasmines wrapped in a newspaper, I freed the flowers from the paper and found a small rose bud tucked in between. When I was busy admiring these flowers when, he walked into the living room, "You like Jasmines. I like the rose." Without a word I ran into the room and showed him the shirt. We both laughed and I coyly wiped off a happy tear before he noticed it.

The next morning was a Sunday. I had pinned the Jasmines and a rose to my hair, and he had worn the shirt I had gifted. We decided to visit the temple, like we always did. But this time the silence didn't hang between us. We walked beside each other and there was no room for anybody to walk in between us. The awkwardness had disappeared, the newness was weaning off. As we boarded the rickety bus and stood huddled together, I rested my hand on my husband's shoulder as if it was the most natural thing to do and that moment I knew we had formed that timeless bond.

P.S: This is written as a part of Captured Writings. The inspiration for this story is the picture.

Thursday, December 15, 2011

The Not So Ordinary Couple

I think it was about four months back. A friend and I were dragging our feet to finish one round of a lake, famous amongst joggers and fitness freaks. The crisp and cold air, the lovely greens, calm sky, sleepy birds and the shimmering water had marked the morning.

It had become a habit to see the usual faces, to unknowingly make a note of their peculiar styles. A man who walked with so much grace— it made a young girl like me jealous. There was a girl who jogged at a pace slower than we walked at, her foot would rise about an inch from the ground and she would give it an act of a jog. Her elbows perpetually stuck to the sides of her body, we wondered why she didn't rather choose to walk? An old lady sat near a bench somewhere about a kilometre from where we started, her paper like skin, soft features and light coloured clothes had a soothing effect. Exchanging some smiles and words was always a pleasure. There was also a really fat guy who jogged as we walked; we drew silent inspiration from him. Though he coyly lowered his head when people passed by—to all of us he was a hero.

There were also others who came and went. Their routine lasted few days and then they disappeared into the small city and we never saw them again at the lake. We didn't care much for these people. But we would smile when we saw the regulars, note if they had lost weight, ran faster, got new company, and wore new attire. Something told me they did the same when they looked at us.

That day was very ordinary, very usual until we saw them—a husband and a wife. I didn't know it for sure, what their relation exactly was but it was something about the way they were that left no room for doubt. They were running at a good pace, not a sluggish jog but proper running. Her shoulder length hair billowed in the light breeze. It gave away a shine of dark golden brown when the sunlight danced upon wisps of her silken tresses. She looked refined and dignified in a well picked pair of running shoes and a comfortable green t-shirt over black tracks. They looked like they were in their mid thirties though with her pretty face and a passing glance she could have been mistaken to be much younger. He was wearing a vibrant yellow t-shirt over dark blue tracks—not a handsome face but charming, covered by an ugly pair of sunglasses.

Their feet moved with unbelievable synchrony. Her foot and his foot landing on the ground at the exact same second and the distance covered by each of their step—fixed—no deviation, no gaps, and no mismatches. They looked fascinating. The man's head was tilted a little upward, like he was looking at the sky and her eyes were fixed on the path with rapt attention. When they came closer we noticed their smiles—genuine and heartfelt. But what we noted next saddened us but also stirred us deep inside. The woman's one hand was fixed in the same position, her right elbow bent at an exact ninety degree angle and the man's hand clutched on to it. The second hand of the lady safe sealed his grip on her hand, to ensure it didn't slip as they ran. The ugly sunglasses of the man suddenly made sense, and didn't look even one bit odd. Before we could get over what we had just witnessed—the not so ordinary couple, the woman and her blind husband disappeared from our sight and we never saw them again.

The End

P.S: Based on a true incident

The Doodle

The bookshelves on the three walls of the room made it look much smaller than it was. There was a big green bulletin board which recklessly covered the only ventilating windows of the room and gave it a damp and dull touch. Apart from the circulars and notices pinned on to the board which flapped and fluttered as the fan swept the air across the room—there was no sound. An old man round and cute with his little head shimmering under the glaze of the tube light propped his glasses while looking at the boy. The boy had turned purple with fear. He curled his lanky legs around the chair and tied his hands behind his back. His face was more sad than apologetic. "It is okay son. I am not going to punish you." the principal tried to free the boy of the tension. The boy murmured, "Sorry!" As soon as a bell rang the boy panicked and stood on his feet. The old man just said, "You may go. Attend your classes and . . . ." and before he could finish his line the boy had disappeared out of the room.

His fat fingers held a paper on which there was a grotesque caricature of him. He was amazed by the representation of his own body. A plump figure with an oversized head, two big droopy ears, a rather flat nose and his shirt sleeves curtly cut by sharp stokes of pencil while the legs disappeared towards the end of the paper. He touched his nose in a reflex and sighed after feeling a slight bump. Not that flat, he thought. He quickly hid the drawing in his desk when someone knocked on the door. It was the purchase officer of the school who wanted to know if they should change the book seller. It had been five years and the contract was nearing expiry. He neatly place three sheets of papers with quotes from different sellers in the city, "Sir? Sir? . . . . Do you want me to come later." The old man twitched his nose and said, "No. So, you were saying . . . ?"

The conversation went on again and again reaching no conclusion. The principal appeared very dazed. He would corner his eyeballs to look at his ears or touch them with his hands he spoke. The officer sat stiff hiding his growing irritation with the man in front of him. He had a grand plan, to favour a seller over the others and pocket a greedy couple of thousands, but let alone questioning about the book sellers the Principal didn't even look at the quotations. He started again, "The Trinetra Book Seller has been over charging us Sir. Since the contract with them will expiry by this January I proactively requested quotations from couple of other book stores in the city. From my analysis . . . ."

He prepared speech was cut short by the old man who now held his hands high holding his ears, bracketing himself within the bent elbows, "Are my ears too big?" The officer was thrown off balance. It took him a while to understand that the guy wasn't making fun of him and was expecting a genuine answer. The Principal's eyes narrowed to put the man in the spot as if he wanted to force a reply out of his mouth. The irritated officer blurted out with an absent mind, "Not your ears but . . . Sir, I always thought you had a big—forehead. Maybe I should come some other time" He excused himself gingerly not knowing what else to do. Soon after the officer left, the old man pulled out the Caricature from his desk and noted the big swoop the boy had made near his forehead. He ran his hands over his face as the doodle snickered back at him. He didn't punish the boy but the boy had punished him unknowingly.

The End

Monday, December 5, 2011

The Maid and The Lady

I was out of work because two of my employers had shifted to some other cities. I had put up a word with the watchman to let me know if any new families moved into these houses. My boundaries were restricted to the Krishna Colony. I was not allowed to work beyond that area. The other maids wouldn't approve of that. There was an untold understanding, all of us were poor and one would become an out-caste if one sabotaged the livelihood of other maids.

On one Thursday I was summoned to meet the Sharma Family. Thursday, I figured it was a blessing from Sai Baba. The last couple of tens carefully preserved in the loose end of my saree would have lasted for couple more days, I needed this job. I washed my face and tied my hair neatly and reached the building where the Sharma's lived. I was apprehensive. It is very difficult to be a maid in these big houses, their strength and money scares me. I feel so vulnerable. Within us maid we all knew it is better to work for families with kids than for bachelors and newlyweds. So, when my doorbell was answered by a ten year old relief comforted my tense body. The girl was sweet. In the first few seconds I could guess she was a well mannered child. She spoke to me with respect. "Aunty, please wait. I'll call mommy." Rich kids sometimes be very harsh, I now had a positive feeling about the lady of the house. A tall, very fair and gorgeous lady walked out of the kitchen, and called me in. The house was littered with cardboard boxes and wrappers. The mother and child spoke to each other in Hindi. They didn't belong to this area of the country. "Please sit"

I noted that she gestured towards the mat that covered one corner of the living room. To my surprise she sat down next me," Will you have tea? I need to drink it before I can do anything. My head is paining. Hands are aching. Why doesn't the lift work in this building?" I soon forgot all the calculations I was making regarding the salary, the woman spoke to with ease and a familiarity I was starting to like. "No." She brought the tea anyway and I sipped the hot ginger tea. I noticed my glass was different than hers. But it didn't matter, we were drinking the same tea and I wasn't offered a left over. "I need you to help me with setting up the house. That is first. And, I need you to help me with the dishes, clothes and cleaning the house. But there is one more problem. I am working. So you will have to come at around 6:30 in the morning. Is that fine?" I noted everything she said but she had left out the one piece of information I badly needed to know—how much is she going pay? "I can come at 6:30, I don't have an issue. I should be able to get done by 8.00. Ma'am, I will accept the standard salary in this colony—100 for dishes, 150 for clothes and 150 for cleaning." It was a done deal and I began with washing the tea cups.

One question nagged me, where was her husband? It was none of my business but she seemed too nice a lady to be di-vorzed. Isn't that what they call it when the man and woman in these big families separate? Months passed and morning tea and breakfast with the lady and her daughter became my routine. The other maids were so jealous, because I got food, hot food and my employer usually sat down and ate with me. On lucky days she would pass on some wonderful clothes that I would fold and keep aside to wear them on special occasions. I was soon hired to come during evenings as well to help her with the cooking, and we chatted about movies and serials. I was growing more and more attached to her little family and it pained me, that they hid a lot of grief beneath smiles.

There were days when I would catch her cry each time she hung up on a particular call. His voice was coarse and harsh, "She has no time to answer the calls and she is taking care of my girl?" I realized my mistake and passed on the phone to her. When she began to scream I excused myself so that she doesn't feel too embarrassed. The next morning she pretended nothing happened. Or, as if it was very casual to fight. I hadn't slept the last night. I kept thinking about her and about her child. I wanted to say a lot of things; I had prepared to speak about myself, about my marriage about my husband who too no longer stays with me. I wanted to tell her to be strong, to stop answering his calls—lodge a police complaint like I did. But, I remained silent—I was her maid and maids are not supposed to speak about families. I would see the little girl's lips quiver with pain and tears welled up her eyes whenever this happened and the otherwise noisy house would drown in the silence of the haunted past. The abandoned cup of tea pushed below her bed, gave away signs of a long painful night. I could visualize her sitting with her back propped to the corner of the bed. Her knees closely drawn and hands cupping the hot tea, the only comforting warmth within her reach. As I made the bed on these days, I flipped the pillows to hide the tears marks; I felt too burdened with that knowledge. I pretended I saw nothing, noticed nothing. She pretended she didn't know that I knew.

I tried to understand the situation from the snippets of information I had over heard by chance when the lady talked to her mother and in-laws. "I made a mistake. I understand. But you cannot take away my child! You get it? Not you, not him, not anyone!" *What had she done?* I wondered. She was very good. It was hard to imagine she would have faulted. She cared for her child more than anything and she was raising the daughter much better than anybody I have worked with. Sadly, we live in a society where people can talk about things they do not know and still not get their tongues chopped off. The other maids told me stuff about her which I knew weren't true. Some thought she was widow, who still unabashedly flaunted her beauty and draped herself in bright colours. Some thought that men frequented her house and that is why her husband had left her alone—Not TRUE. I knew, it. She made an attempt to be lively, she is a good person by nature, I could tell but then—there was something the woman had wronged. Something she didn't forgive herself for. She was in pain. When they asked me questions about her—"I just do my work. I find her to be good. I know nothing else." That was my reply. I felt bad for her. What did they know about her to talk about her like that?

This work had become my stable source of income. I got two meals a day and respect? And more than anything, I connected to her. I saw through her. Don't get into their personal business. Do your work and leave. Wasn't that what every maid was once told? But that fateful day I crossed my line. As I walked closer to the house, the door was ajar; I heard the voice of man, a familiar voice. I hesitated to step in, maybe I should just leave, it was a family matter and they wouldn't appreciate my presence. One final thought was to pull the door closer, neighbours weren't too fond of her, and the fight might just give them a reason to push the lady out of the building. As I reached out for the door the little girl ran towards me, to my horror a moderately built man was overpowering the lady and his hand was strangling her neck. In a reflex, I lifted the little statue that stood on the table and hit it on his head. The man dropped unconscious. The daughter ran to her and the mother and child rolled into a ball in the corner. The lady never looked at me; I didn't want to see her in such a weak position either. I called the police and gave my statement. The man was left with a warning as the lady had refused to file a case. However, he was bound by law not call at this house or get anywhere close to his once daughter and wife. When the tension faded, I was afraid—what if I would lose my job. People can act in weird ways. What if even she would? I dreaded to hear that one statement, "Who are you to do that?"

After about two weeks, she handed me a generous amount only to let me know, they were shifting to a new place. The society had seen enough and thought that she was nuisance. It is strange how the community can act so stupid collectively. Hadn't the woman been through enough? I helped her pack her things. Each time I looked at her face which was still red by the scars from that ghastly day, I wanted to tell her, "whatever, you have done—forgive yourself. That man has done something worse than anything you would have done. Be strong. Be strong." I held back my tears and didn't let a word slip. As we sipped our last cup of tea, she suddenly blurted out," I had stepped outside my marriage once. I thought I deserved to die." I couldn't stop myself anymore," What is a woman to do when she lives with a man like that?"

Those were our last words. She just held my hand and hugged me like I was her sibling. "Aunty, Thank you" just these three words from the sweet child justified all the risk I took. She didn't deserve to lose her mother. I kissed her goodbye. Soon after they left, I walked back to the watchman," Let me know when some new family moves into that house."

The End

The Movie

That scene never left my mind—chilly breeze, her hair floating in the air, dressed perfectly looking so damn beautiful, her mind unsure—her heart beating wild and he grabs her and swings her into his arms and looks right into her eyes—Oh . . . his blue eyes! And, that's their moment. That moment when two people know, they are meant to be, now and forever. After living that high, waiting with bated breath,—I sulked, walked out on my boyfriend with a lame excuse. It is too harsh for a woman to be crashed into the real world after a two hour fairytale dream. The credits roll and you realise it was just a story.

When the movie ended, it seemed inappropriate to be holding the hand of a guy with pop-corn stuffed in his mouth. I mean look at that charming man on the screen, and how wonderful is the story of that couple. I couldn't help but get sucked into the dream they sold to me, two hours and I despised my whole reality. "Hey, are we grabbing dinner at Chelo's?" he asked with the predictability of routine that built between us over our five months of dating. But, just at that precise second I felt like he is a growing appendix that my body is rejecting, and if I don't cut him off now, I could burst. "I don't feel too well." I pretend nausea and land up at home earlier than planned.

I think about this guy, I think about us—nothing special, just casual, two random people—run into each other, meet, date, talk, and go around—no defining moment. If I think of putting up a song track to our love life—it would be a Nothing! No passion, no wild love, no craze, just two level headed people finding compatibility. With a mouthful of chocolate ice-cream to satiate my remorse I stare blankly into the wall. It starts to rain and it makes me feel worse. How I wish I'd walk out to find a handsome young man getting drenched in the rain to catch a glimpse of me—like Mr. Andrew in the movie. It is pathetic! What do these movies do to us? I wonder what the inspiration to these movies is—It is no way a reality, it is not! I bury my face in the pillow to continue to dream, to prolong that effect of the movie.

The bright sky greets me and I refuse to wake up, pull over the sheets above my head and tuck myself in. A message blinks right into my eye. "Pick you up in 20mins. Hope you feeling better." I drag myself out of the bed and focus my thoughts on work. With few sips of coffee I run down the stairs, my mind still hung over and delusionary. I find him waiting at my door. "You are feeling better?" I nod my head and we walk. The traffic is bustling; the city is living up to its Monday morning jams. I feel unsure, as if an alarm went off in my head, I walk blindly—thinking about a *break up?* In the next few seconds I feel his hand grab mine and pull me back. "**Watch out lady!**" an angry voice screams from the car that almost ran over me. Little shaken I look at a simple man, a silly simple man, holding me as if I am the most loved person in this world. His heart is beating with the fear of almost losing me. As he hugs me shielding from what could have been I feel secure—no passion, no craze—just lot of love and care. All of my senses tune to him—I breathe in his life, his love, his presence. I could be nowhere else; I could be with nobody else. This is our fairytale moment, the defining moment—it is real, it is him. The movie is—so surreal and funny. Reality is now—my high!

The End

Waiting in the Dark

The city with all its glitz and lights was dazzling in the night. But the lights were somewhere in the background, as if an uptown New York night view wallpaper was pasted far away. Patches of road appeared and disappeared synchronized with the limited throw of headlights as the vehicles swished by. The flickering street lights reduced the visages of people to black unfamiliar contours only giving a hint of their faces from the momentary flashes of light. Here I was a thirty year old lady, near the bus stand in the outskirts of a city, waiting in the dark. I cursed the man who had loved me dearly for the past five years for this delay of five minutes. I frantically tried to reach him on his mobile, failing at which I dropped some angry messages while actually trying to take of my mind off the surroundings and seem occupied.

My eyes bounced from one person to another. A little fear crept in each time I saw the silhouette, of a man. I checked the time, it was a little past nine thirty. A lump rose to my throat and stomach twisted. The voice of my mother during my teenage days came back like an unexpected echo, shaking me, reminding of all the horrors that can happen in the dark. To wipe out the thoughts and feel a little secure I hopped and stood near a lady almost five years younger to me. It was a relief, acknowledging the presence of another woman. With a new found strange courage I looked at the men around us, seeing them for the first time with a neutral eye. They were no different than the men I meet on day to day basis. A hardworking middle aged guy with his bag strap stashed across his chest, a moody typical teenage student, a day worker starching his hair, deciding on puffing a beedi tucked into multiple turns of red and yellow sacred thread wrapped around his wrist.

While this sudden knowledge of common men set out waves of comfort, black thoughts still nagged my mind snubbing the possibility of respite. The horror stories of molestation, rape, kidnapping, abuse kept hovering over my head like cursing demons. Where the hell was my

128

husband? It is unlike him, to be this late. Now an additional fear splashed in my already turbulent mind. Finally a message beeped and I was informed my guy was stuck in the nasty traffic due to a harsh accident. It does seem like a bad day for many people—*harsh accident?* My eyes glued to the mobile screen I try not to look around and make an eye contact with these common men. A rapist doesn't roam with a board indicating the same—it could be anybody. With impulse I turn my head around to confirm a noisy brawl between two men walking towards the stand where we stood, we—me, the younger lady and the strange men. Two men in drunken madness, screaming and clearly out of their senses—my stomach touches the ground. With one of the other million pre-programmed reflexes built in every woman, we two ladies step closer and stand next to each other as if we were childhood friends.

Why should I fear? I chide myself. Really coming to senses for the first time since I stepped into this bare corner of the street, stripped from the comfort of daylight and facing strangely expose fears which came to light in this darkness, waiting for my husband to take me back to my safe home. I can scream, my nails are uncut, the jeans is comfortable to raise my foot crotch high with required amount of force, I have a police number in my speed dial, I have a strong fist too and the lady beside me, of course she would help, now why wouldn't she? But, all these fall flat when I look at the time again—fifteen past ten. If I ever want to get rid of my husband all I need to do is mention this incident to my mother. *Past ten!*

As if my worries were less, the day worker starts roaming about the place breaking through the invisible divide we woman made near the where we stood. My heart hopped into my mouth, when he tried to ask something in some incomprehensible language, with a sheepish smile plastered across his face. I walk away in a quick movement making a disgusted brave face but am actually scared like a little abandoned child, fully aware of the ugliness of the world. The worker walks away mumbling and I realize probably he didn't mean any harm, maybe just too dazed with the tired day, beedi puffs or maybe some desi daaru, I pinch my nose as he leaves a trail of odour behind him. Of course he could do harm, anyone could be harmful, men drunk, not drunk, educated, uneducated, upper class, lower class—there was nothing that clearly separated the good from the bad. And all you need to be in that vulnerable spot is be a woman, nothing matters, the clothes, the decency, the looks, age—nothing really.

A shrill horn breaks my endless symphony with the stressful night. I hop into the car with great relief . . .

For happy ending—

. . . shoot an angry look at my husband. I slam the door and look at the stand where I stood nearly for an hour fearing my life as a woman. I look at the lady, my companion in the joint misery. I stop my husband from shifting the gear and tell him," Let's wait till someone comes to pick her up." He turns the key and the engine hum mutes abruptly. The young woman walks and stands closer to our car with the deepest sense of gratitude and we share a smile exchanging our identities for the first time.

For twisted ending—

. . . sit in and slam the door in a hurry. I pull out my handkerchief and wipe the beads of fear off my face. While a couple of kilometres away I prop my head on the car window to gaze back the horror I lived through. I notice a car similar to our halt at the stop. Suddenly this car feels strange below my feet. The dashboard doesn't have the Ganesh idol, the seat covers are a shade darker, the foot rug is missing . . . I fear looking at what monster could be seated in the driver's seat next to me. How blindly fearful was I? My phones rings and—it is my husband calling.

THE END

P.S: It is strange how just one para about 100 words can change the whole track of the story and change how it makes the reader feel. Hope you cherish this little experiment as much as I did writing it. :)

The Coin Collection-Part1

Asha hobbled her way to the kitchen where she usually found her mother during the mornings. She rubbed her eyes adjusting them to the light that pierced her. Her tiny feet touched the ground and waves of tingling sensations made her feel funny. A soft white cotton gown with fading red flower prints made her look adorable. Her hair bounced, recovering from the twists and twirls they had been subjected in her sleep and the faint pillow prints still showed on her cheeks. Without opening her eyes she clung on to her mom who was pulling out some bags. "Did you brush your teeth?" she asked. To which Asha whimpered as if that question ruined her morning.

In a hurried tone her mom said, "Oh, okay! So you can't come with me then. Since, you haven't brushed your teeth." With these lines she had managed to zap the early morning melancholy between her and her sleepy lazy daughter who she knew hated to brush. Now wide awake Asha tugged her mom, "Where are you going amma? I will come with you. Pl-ea-se!" Her mother had replied," But, I don't have the time. If you brush in five minutes we will see!" Asha quickly disappeared into the bathroom and came out with a wet face and little toothpaste foam she had managed to spill on her gown. Her mom helped her changed her clothes and they left for the vegetable market.

Asha liked to accompany her mother on all her purchases. Unlike appa who wouldn't budge on her desire to buy a toffee or two her mom would make sure she got some goodies. There were times when she got balloons and a big chocolate bar with a purple wrapper. It was usually during the first week of every month. Her mom had once explained it to her," Amma got her salary, Asha." She had spent the whole day trying to spell it," Sa-la-ury."

They made the usual stops at the same vendors, like they did every week. "Madam, today grapes are very nice. Take a kilo or two. Taste them, don't buy if you don't like them" the fruit vendor plucked a couple of grapes and placed them in Asha and her mom's hand. Little reluctant she looked at her mom and popped into her mouth after her mom did the same. They bought half a kilo and moved ahead to finish the remaining shopping. At every seller they stopped, there was an exchange of notes and a slipping of coin or two after some bargaining. Her mom handed over these coins to Asha as she struggled with the now heavy bags dragging them from one stop to another. Sometimes more coins were added and Asha had to fill them in her frill gown pockets and sometimes she dutifully searched the one or two rupee her mom would need and promptly handed it over on request.

There was a sense of ownership for the money. But she knew that money belonged to her mother. She secretly hoped that her mom wouldn't require the change and she could go home with her two tiny pockets—full of coins. Her mom never insisted on collecting back the coins from her. But, Asha would ask if she could add the change to her piggy bank to which she would not be given a negative answer. Asha would sit on the floor and pile up her coins in batches of ones and twos and estimate the money she had. It was a action she had picked up from the Uncle Scroog cartoons and dreamt of swimming in a pool of coins someday. She never understood why the coins on television were golden and yellow while all the coins she had ever seen were only grey. "Why do you save these coins?" her mother had asked her once. She didn't have an answer. She didn't know anything about money. She just replied," I feel good amma. I like to pile them up and count them. I will be Uncle Scroog!"

When they came back from the vegetable market, Asha asked the same question and quickly ran into her room and added the twelve coins she had in her pocket to her collection.

Note: Yes! You read it correct. There is a Version 2 for part-2 of the story continued . . . . Hang on till the new Part-3 and let me know which one you like.

The Coin Collection-Part2

Asha's mom was amazed at the dedication of the little girl to save money she knew nothing about. How innocently she dreams, Uncle Scroog! She wiped a happy tear from corner of her eye before it rolled out on her cheek. The rest of the afternoon went by cooking the lunch, talking to the maid, catching up with the Sunday serials and handing out cups of hot coffee to her husband. "It is not hot enough" he would flatly refuse, returning the cup to her and she would repeat the process till it was boiling hot. "It is too hot now. Why can't you make a cup of coffee?" he would get angry. Thoughts rushed through her mind; a faint familiar feeling of pain strained her. Was he punishing her, proving to her that she wasn't good enough a wife? What is so wrong about a woman earning better than the man she lives with. What is that futile Ego? And where was that pride when he had rummaged through her cupboard? When he robbed his own wife of the meagre hundred, two hundred she had carefully placed between the ironed saree folds.

But then why did *she* feel guilty? She couldn't even look him in the eye. It was not fear. Definitely not fear. It was perhaps—disgust. And, the guilt, the woman was burdened by it the day she was born. She felt guilty when her parents spent even that final rupee of their savings on her wedding. She felt guilty about being beautiful, about attracting too much attention. About being looked at with endearing eyes by strange men while her husband felt nothing! On one drunken night he had confessed," I can't bear you being so strong. You make me feel miserable about myself. Why can't you just be a bloody woman?" She had thought of talking it out discussing it but she held her tongue. The following morning she pretended nothing had happened and he played along, life slipped into the same miserable rut. There were nights when she watched Asha sleep; thinking what would happen to her future. How will she ever earn enough to pay for her college? Would she ever have that kind of money?

"Amma, am-ma come see my box it is full!" Asha pulled the loose end of her mom's saree, while bouncing in the air," Come, Co-me, Co-me Amma . . . see it is fu-ull!" Much to her delight, the little girl did manage to fill the box. Later that evening they went to a nearby shop and got it changed to crisp notes. The final count was a hundred and twenty three, a priceless saving of her eight year old. She carefully rolled the hundred rupee note and tucked it under the paper of Asha's coin box. She pulled out some loose change and threw them in," Here you go Asha, now you can collect again!"

It took Asha four years before the exact value of rupee got into her head. Four years to grow out of that innocence, look around know how strangely rich and poor they were. Appa had these bouts of lavishness and he filled the house with fridge, a washing machine and a fancy colour television. She would believe they were rich enough to afford these luxuries. But then later she would hear amma cry and speak to her appa," I can't pay for this. We have a little girl to educate! You know how they talk when they come to collect the money for all the debt you have created? I am begging you. Stop! It is enough." She had asked her mom on one such dark night," Amma, why can't we pay them the money I have? You won't have to listen to them" Her mother shot an angry glance, almost terrified at the thought," Never even mention about spending that money. I know it is hard. But don't ever do that! Whatever happens . . ."

"Whatever happens . . . ?" did Amma just say that! Asha choked on these words and tear welled up her eyes. She turned her face away and secretly wiped the tears on her t-shirt sleeves. Her mother sensed her discomfort. She hugged the girl and wept mumbling between sobs," I didn't mean that. It is all going to be fine. I will be fine. We will be fine. Nothing is going to happen to me."

That night when Asha cried, something changed. Her mother had realized how much pressure it was on a child who is twelve. She felt miserable that she had no plan, no idea no way figured out. All she knew was the money could be put to some use when Asha grew up. She thought about it the whole night. Her mind was suddenly occupied with a thought that had never crossed her mind. There was a strange excitement about this thought. "What if?" she caught herself wondering and shuddered at the possibilities. Helplessness burdened her. There is no place for a woman who walks out on her man. But could she just disappear into the darkness and never see him again? What about Asha? She couldn't leave her behind. Tears poured as she snubbed the thought of killing herself and the daughter to end it all. "No, I will never do that. I will be a bloody woman if I do."

When Asha got up the next morning, she found her mom in the kitchen, as usual. But there was something different about her. She had never seen Amma like this ever before. She handed the coffee cup to Appa before he even asked for it. She added a couple of biscuits too. It all felt awkward. Amma had always had this look of a warrior; there was a subtle anger in everything she did, a sublime display of strength and resentment in her eyes. But, today she appeared like nothing touched her. There was no emotion, just a faint smile when she looked at Asha.

Little worried Asha left to school. Her mom had waved her and there was the faint smile again. She had to have faith in Amma. She thought about all the decisions Amma could take, did she decide we leave this place and settle far away from appa? She was a strong lady, but would she do that? She had never thought about it in all these years. Paralysed with thoughts she sat inattentive. "Asha? Asha? You need to go." She shook from her thoughts when the teacher called out to her. "What happened?" she asked. "Your mother . . . your mother . . ." the lady was struggling to find words. An intense pain rushed thought her heart," What happened to my mother? Please!" The teacher finally spoke" Your mother is in the hospital. She is fine. But you need to go"

Asha jumped off from her school van and ran in the first direction she saw. She wanted to kill Appa. How could he? He was horrible but she always thought he couldn't harm them—physically. She knew he couldn't. How could he? A peon from the school who had accompanied her directed her to the room 306. She saw lot of police uniforms. She didn't know what to expect. She gulped down nasty thoughts nagging her mind and walked in. She found Amma, wrapped in bandages. One hand was in fracture plaster and her left leg was hung high. Her cheekbone was swollen and her face was red. There was a needle stuck to her arm and transparent liquid dripped. She sat next to her not knowing what else to do. Amma was sleeping. But there was a faint smile. She was beginning to wonder when the police officer called her," Asha. I want you to answer a few questions. Your mother will be fine. She will recover soon. Can you talk to me now?" Asha looked at Amma and nodded. The officer asked her," Think properly and tell me, could your father do this?" Asha turned around in disbelief. She looked at that faint smile on Amma's face. She knew the truth. But she wanted sound unsure," I think Appa did it." The officer questioned her further," Why would he do that? Can you remember anything happened yesterday or today morning?" By now she made up her mind she looked Amma, her faint smile. She had to have faith in her. She framed an answer and lied," Appa did it. Amma and me used to save money—some coins. Appa wanted Amma to give him that money. They were fighting about it all the while—about *the coin collection*."

P.S: Did the story move as expected? Did it take a nasty turn? Do find it believable? Any complaints? Any suggestions . . . ? I am all ears.

The coin collection—Part2
[2nd Version]

**(the first para is same as the first version—
it changes from the second para)**

Asha's mom was amazed at the dedication of the little girl to save money. What did she know about money? How innocently she dreams, Uncle Scrooge! She wiped a happy tear from the corner of her eye before it rolled out on her cheek. The rest of the afternoon went by in cooking the lunch, talking to the maid, catching up with the Sunday serials and handing out cups of hot coffee to her husband. "It is not hot enough" he would flatly refuse, returning the cup to her and she would repeat the process till it was boiling hot. "It is too hot now. Why can't you make a cup of coffee?" he would get angry. Thoughts rushed through her mind; a faint familiar feeling of pain strained her. Was he punishing her, proving to her that she wasn't good enough a wife, now because she is working? What is so wrong about a woman earning better than the man she lives with. What is that futile Ego? And where was that pride when he had rummaged through her cupboard? When he robbed his own wife of the meagre hundred, two hundred she had carefully placed between the ironed saree folds?

She only hoped and prayed that he would leave Asha's coins untouched. "Amma, am-ma come see my box it is full!" Asha pulled the loose end of her mom's dress, while bouncing in the air," Come, Co-me, Co-me Amma . . . see it is fu-ull!" She quickly shushed her and followed her to the room. Much to her delight, the little girl did manage to fill the box. Later that evening they went to a nearby shop and got it changed to crisp notes. The final count was a hundred and twenty three, a priceless saving of her eight year old. She carefully rolled the hundred rupee note and tucked it under the paper of the coin box. She pulled out some loose change from her purse," Here you go Asha, now you can collect again!"

An innocent child has the eyes that can see people without bias. Asha was no different. She would hop around with delight and tell her father;" Appa I saved two rupees" It was only after several reckless remarks that she had started to ignore his presence. How knowledge can rob away some senseless happiness? Nobody asked her to but she had learned to tip-toe and make sure the coins didn't juggle enough to catch the attention of Appa. "Did you save a Rupee?" he would snicker at her. She would hang her head down in anger and do the bravest thing a child of her age could do. She ran to her mother. "Don't let him bother you. Here take a rupee." Amma always managed to patch the cracks made by Appa in Asha's illusion of a happy childhood. But, Asha, she was maturing at a remarkable rate.

She would startle her mother with some blunt questions," Amma, why does Appa not like money?" Amma would feel guilty of all that Asha could have overheard. Could she tell her that it was only *her money* that he didn't like? Asha knew nothing other than Appa throwing a bundle of tens on the floor shouting," Take that money! I can earn well enough!" She had crawled under the bed believing that it was a bad dream. With gentle sobs and anxious eyes she had waited till she saw Amma's feet walk in. She jumped into her arms and had embraced her with a delight of not having lost her. There was this strange fear about Appa. She always thought her could hurt her mother. Maybe it was from watching Amma cry whenever Appa spoke to her. The best advice her young mind could offer was," We should stay at Ajji's house. Appa never comes there". How simplistic was Asha's comprehension of the complex life around her. Her mother feared the day when see would see things deeper and clearer.

A woman is like that string that holds different relations in a marriage. If she breaks off, all the beads fall apart. What is the victory in that—to run away?

But who would explain this complexity of an Indian marriage to Asha. Who would tell her that her mother grew up listing to how she should endure all that a wedding had to offer. And that the ones who walked away were cowards, women who didn't know how to deal with a man! Could she understand what it meant to be a girl child of a broken family?

Their life had slipped into a melancholic rut. And they were too careful not to step into each other's life. Father—one of Asha's foundation bonds was reduced to middle aged stranger who lived under the same roof. She learned to hold back her questions and wait for the life to unfold itself. Wait, because a worry seemed to trouble her. Situation was strangely comfortable. Why lash out a ripple in still water?

Her mother had looked like a warrior two years ago with a trace of resentment in whatever she did for her father. But now the image was fading, the helplessness of Amma surfaced. When she looked at Amma, Asha would blame herself for all the complications. Docile Amma would never have set her foot out to work had it not been for Asha. Probably she wouldn't have had any complaints with the man whom she calls a husband. The mutual silence in the family made her think beyond her age. There were many nights when she cried herself to sleep. She flipped the pillow around to hide the tear marks, what if Amma sees it? After all Amma still believed Asha had nothing but just a faint idea of the trouble. Amma believed she had mastered masking the harsh reality. Why break her heart?

The coin box was full and it was time to get it changed to notes. Few years ago, there was cheer about the money. Asha would jump with glee and clap her hands when they got the coins changed. A joy that was meaningless. Today she was silent, when Amma and she walked to the nearby grocery. "So, that is a lot of money! You will become Uncle Scrooge if you continue this way." her mother tried to make a conversation. Asha looked giving an infinitely mature look to her mother passed a smile that usually mothers' pass to an innocent children. Amma was taken aback. She tried to cheer up the girl, pointing out to general life around them, a cute little baby, a new fancy building, a sleepy dog, an over burdened motor vehicle, but none had an effect on the girl. She walked with rapt attention. Her mind fixed elsewhere.

Asha had, looked at people and learned the difference in the life of other kids and hers. She had looked at families with the child holding the parents in union. It pained her, these observations. Amma had started to worry about the changes Asha had been displayed. Like the girl was carrying a thought too heavy for her delicate mind. *"Don't let it get to you head, stay atop, ignore, and be in that melancholic rut . . ."* but she didn't say a word. This is not the time.

The grocery store man passed a practiced smile with perfection. He looked at little Asha and spoke to her mother," Madam, this girl will become lakhpati very soon!" Amma turned to Asha proud of her young daughter's accomplishment. The man carefully counted the coins counting the stacks of ten rupees he had made with Asha's coins. "Here you go, two hundred and thirty, what will you do with all that coin collection, buy nice toys?" the man asked as he handed over the notes to Asha. "Amma was about to respond back—"She wants to be Uncle Scro . . ." when Asha spoke with a tinge of irritation," No, with that coin collection, I want to get away from home—far away from Appa". While the man pretended to get busy with other customers a unfazed little girl in her frilled cotton gown and shocked Amma walked back home in silence.

Two mothers

"Please, please! Drop me one message—once you reach fine. Can you do that for me?" I hear my mother snicker, as I talk to my little girl. I throw a furious look at her and she bends her head down like punished a child. After finishing the talk and waving my daughter a goodbye, I join mom at the dining table where she tries to appear engrossed in cutting vegetables. Her silvery, shoulder length stylishly cut hair, bounces with the chop of the knife. There is a smile she is pressing between her lips. My anger vanishes and we both burst out laughing.

Overjoyed, little tears flow and rub them off still laughing. A little nagging thought attaches to my mind. I abruptly stop. She reads my mind," *Oh dear! No . . . you will do fine!*" and walks to where I sat. Burying my face in her embrace I mumble without looking at her, "*Mom, why is it so difficult to be a mother?*" She gently kisses my forehead," Because I cursed you to have a difficult child, as difficult and as painful as you were." We both laugh. "Now don't think so much you silly." with those words she hobbles to the TV room and switches the television on. I wait for her to say the same words she says every day," Aye, which channel does that show telecast on?" With practice, I answer," Channel 15." If I ask her now, about the guy who had chased me till house some fifteen years ago, Pat, she will reply. But a TV show she watches daily, she won't remember its channel or even its exact name. That's how the memory of a mother works.

I walk into kitchen and start to cook. When she says," Put the tomato in the end. They fry very quickly." I tell her I saw her doing just that all my life. "I am delighted; I never knew you paid attention." she laughs. This was one of those skills I had picked up sitting on the kitchen slab passing this and that to her when she cooked. I shake myself to the present and place the cooked food on the table and check the time. It's been a while. She should have reached by now. I look at the empty message inbox and a chain of thoughts jail me. I feel weak and vulnerable, suddenly exposed to pain. Has she reached safe? There are so many accidents these days. What about those stupid men who will be gawking at her? What if she got into a fight? What if she had started an argument with someone? Yesterday there was a molestation case reported in the similar area. A message beeps, "*Mom, reached safe. Don't worry.*" My mind is out of shackles now. What a relief! That one word—safe, is what I wanted to hear, like every other mother.

We eat and I listen to mom's version of the serials she watches and smile wide eyed at what she believes will be told in the following episodes. Time passes and other members of the family have come, everybody except—my daughter. I can't sit in my own house. I sit in the veranda, my eyes scanning every girl on a Scooty that even remotely resembles her. My ears all alert to pick the noises that usually precede her arrival at home. I drop her message," Let me know if you got held up by something." But, fail to get a reply. As my worry worsens with every passing second, my mom offers me company and we wait for my daughter like she had once waited for me. "Her class might have got extended. And they don't allow mobiles in the class. She told me that once. She must be on her way." She tells me this and yet I catch that little pray she does, hoping this is what is true. "I am hoping the same mom. I am hoping the same." I reply holding back a million insane thoughts haunting my mind. *Times change, generations' change, our attitudes, our lifestyles, everything change! Everything—but that span of time, when you wait for the arrival of a little girl you want to shield from this bad world. That little girl you want to protect for all the horrors you have heard, all the cruelties you have read or have unfortunately witnessed. That time when we the contemporary women, bear the same mindset of every mother who has ever lived. That time—never changes.*

A little later a tiny yellow headlight peeks through our front gate and I breathe for the first time in an hour. *We, two mothers watch 'the daughter' walk towards us—safe and share a smile.*

The End

A Senseless Insecurity

I had been running away from my college memories. But today they hit me like an arrow in the back. I logged onto facebook, it was a lazy Sunday afternoon. There was nothing better to do and I decided to deal with the pending friend requests. Some I confirmed right away, little unsure I left some unattended, a few I bluntly ignored. But this one request, I accepted with lot of hesitation and reluctance. It was a classmate from my graduation days.

I had started hating myself back then, because of this one guy. Arvind Tripathi, the name sounds pretty normal but he was a charm. His wit and smartness had caught the attention of all, including mine. Being the little wise and rational girl I was—I could differentiate between a general liking, an infatuation and love. I was positive and still am sure that I just liked and admired the young man for how he carried himself. I often found myself battling this need that had captured my mind. I wanted a friend. A friend as witty and as cool as him, a rational mind to talk to, and, we did talk for a while.

Suddenly he had withdrawn. Not only that, he refused to acknowledge my presence and say a simple hello. I had spiralled into emotional labyrinths analysing what had gone wrong. I was a blunt, straight forward, no bullshit girl and I never saw any reason for anybody else to be otherwise. Why couldn't he just tell what's wrong? I needed to know. I had even confronted him once to which he gave a *how dumb can you be* smile and walked off. It had stayed with me for days—that disgusted look on his face. Finally, after loathing myself for almost stalking the guy and nearly begging for his company I snapped. I decided to hold my self-respect high. I too ignored him refusing to see his face or respond to any general queries. I hated him for being hurtful. I even deleted his number and removed him from the friends list on social networking sites. It seemed like a brave achievement at seventeen.

Even after that day, I always questioned myself, pondering maybe, I wouldn't have behaved appropriately. Perhaps I clung onto him too much, gave him a wrong impression. Did I like him? I did. But I don't anymore. Did I love him? I didn't. I never did. But it mattered, because I, I was ignored and I wasn't told why. For the rest of the college years—I had learnt to be little aloof, giving space to people, sometimes more than they require. I never entertained many friends. I didn't need them. But once I moved out of college I bounced back to normalcy with ease and learnt a worthy lesson or two. Yet still, *college* became that word which reminded me of my dumbness in dealing with people and made me feel less sure about myself. It wasn't a pleasant memory.

This was that discomforting time of my past I never wanted to think about. But, today out of the blue—like a disowned memory always does, it strayed into my present and itched my mind. I wondered—why now, after ten years Mr. Arvind Tripathi needs to have *me* on his friend list? Was I a puncture to be patched in his list of friends that he suddenly felt the need to deal with? My anger raged and I changed my mind about adding him and was about to block him out when, a messaged popped up.

Hey Aditi,

Sorry, for being the person I was. God knows why I was like that college. You were more sensible than me back then. I feel terrible about how I behaved. So how are you? What are you up to?

Arvind

And there it was—all I had wanted to know. It wasn't *all* my fault. I was not as stupid as I thought I was. There still are a few things I wished I never did. But, I can live with that. *We all are, in our own ways a little unprepared for every situation and stage of life. How easily we feel miserable without the knowledge of who and what the person is all about—burdening ourselves with self doubts.* I felt bad about myself all this while but he in turn was regretful about how he had been. We both felt that the other had handled the situation/college better. It became all clear at once. Like I needed mine, he needed a closure too. A reply, saying—"its okay." or "I understand" was all he wanted. An eternal peace rushed through me as my senseless insecurity, harboured over years disappeared from the dark corners of my mind.

I re-read his message with a smile and logged off without responding.

Sunday, October 16, 2011

The Silhouettes

It still looked the same as it did a year ago. The waves still shimmered as the sun lingered clumsily on the greying sky. There were the usual sounds—a melancholic overlap of laughter, conversations, some hawkers and, most soothing of all, the gushing waves. And then, there were silhouettes—few young, few old, some lovingly coupled and some miserably lonely—lonely, like her. She longed to step into this withdrawing day and become a faceless counter, a shadow on this beach. Disappear away—like *him*.

Here she was, after a year of inconsolable sobbing, denial of *his* absence and accepting the *unfair* life. Her life, at the this moment, was defined by the profile of woman—hands folded, neatly resting above closely drawn knees, the outline of her face looking at the beach. Her hair flowing freely and her mind knotted with thoughts and memories-just another silhouette with a story. It was here that she had found *him*, a few years ago. From a blurred black image of a stranger, *he* had moved into her life—filling it with all colours of joy she could have imagined. She held back tears that threatened to break into an outpour of everything she had deeply shut. An unbearable pain rushed through her body. A boulder of grief shattered her like it had happen just yesterday. Destiny had wiped *him* out of her life cruelly. The dreams they had built together like gleeful children, collapsed overnight. She felt a stab as she watched the kids build sand castles," *Don't*, it won't stay." She wanted to warn.

It was then that her thoughts were suddenly interrupted. She felt the eyes of a stranger glance upon her. She fidgeted uneasily embarrassed about being caught in a private movement. She stared blankly at the beach still cautions of the man, trying hard not to look at him. She felt *weak, vulnerable* and *strangely exposed*. But he stood there adamant, his eyes still caught on her. She emptied the sand from her sandals and in one hurried movement got up and started to walk away. He followed. Her heart paced and her feet dug deep into sand as she ran, slowly, awkwardly,

145

not wanting to give away her fear. For a minute she contemplated about stopping and confronting him. But then she heard him call her, "*Please, wait! Wait . . .* a minute. I need to thank you."

She stopped and turned to find the middle aged man run towards her. She saw his face now, he looked dignified and there was genuine look which kept her from running away. Catching breath while puffing and panting he spoke," I am sorry, You don't know me. I . . . I wanted to give you this." She took the photograph from him with trembling hands. He continued," I had clicked this about a year ago. I have been trying to find you both since then. I am a photographer. And this photograph has become one of my most appreciated works. I wanted to thank you and gift you this. I bring it with me every day. And finally, I saw you now. I wasn't sure at first. But then . . ." he stopped as he saw her cry with joy and pain, her eyes never moved from the photograph. She looked at it dearly and clung to it like a scared child to a mother. Unsure what to say he finally said," *I am sorry . . . I didn't mean to*"

Without a word she hugged him with the deepest sense of gratitude, her gentle sobs with a dash of laugh confused him. He let her hold him not knowing what to do. She loosed the embrace and spoke hugging the photograph close to her heart, "*This . . . this is the biggest joy that I have felt in my life THANK YOU. I have no words to express how grateful I am. He died the night this photograph was taken. This was our last moment together*". The man was so moved he only managed to mumble in a muffled voice," I am *so* sorry to hear about that." They, two strangers, now connected by a mutual grief sat down and wept—two black contours on the magnificent beach.

Later that week she got the photograph beautifully framed. It was a silhouette of a couple, *him* and her holding hands and walking, with *him* leading her and guiding her as the sun silently withdrew throwing a golden light on the beach-the photographer had put up an apt caption," *I will walk you through darkness-forever.*" She had found her strength to live by.

Wednesday, October 12, 2011

Old Friends

"Oh my God! This is you! How are you dear? It's so nice to finally meet you. Long time!! Long long time! Ten years?" I only manage to nod my head with a heartfelt smile. The words I had planned to speak feel heavy on my tongue as she spoke everything I had decided to say when I meet her.

We sit down for a cup a coffee at Barista. I let her place the order for both of us. Too embarrassed to have received a call she excuses herself politely and walks a few steps away. From where I sat her face is just the way it was in my memory several years ago. The only difference being how her hair has grown beautifully long adding more charm to her pretty face. I watch her pace up and down speaking animatedly. Her eyes dart my direction and her muted lips speak," I am sorry" she hasn't changed much—I catch myself smiling at the thought.

I was surprised by this invitation. She had written—"I know . . . It's been so long!! I am finally in your city. Let's catch up!" It is not that I hadn't been in touch with her. But we had slipped to a stage where we both were too busy with our lives. There was a lot to talk, always, but there was never a time and place where this talking could be done. I accepted the growing distance and we were reduced to friends who just call on birthdays. *And, the dreams, the talks and innocent confessions of the school girls that we were back then, feel unfamiliar and odd. Odd, like those old photographs in weird clothes and funny unformed faces that we hide coyly from people who know us today.* I have changed, my dreams have changed, my priorities too. And I know that she too has drifted away from what she had wanted to be.

A worry wraps itself around me. I don't want her to spill out the details of the girl I *had* been to the woman I *have* become. What if she finds my weak, fearful soul while she reaches out the dauntless ambitious girl I was? Did she too change from the perky free spirited girl to a mature woman with a family, career and responsibilities? Would she understand if I break down, unable to hide the grief of my stalling

147

marriage? Would she respond with the concern of that loving friend or would she cringe away in disgust—disappointed with me when I explain the helplessness that led to my now nonexistent career?

My thoughts break with the aroma of freshly brewed coffee. I am shocked to see her sitting right across me. I was so lost I never saw her walk back towards where I sat. In an attempt to conceal the thoughts printed on my face I hide behind the coffee mug. I make a futile effort to clam my apprehensions by sipping the caffeine and try to appear casual. I manage to surface a smile, while still looking away when I feel her eyes glance upon me. Tears threaten to roll down my cheeks and I feel her hands grab mine in the most reassuring manner. Comfort soothes my tensed body. I finally find the courage to look into her eyes and they speak out to me. That moment I know, *she knows—she understands.* The ten years of no communication shatters with this silent, wordless conversation.

The End

Revathi

"Here is your seat. Call Ramesh when you reach Bangalore. I have given him the coach details. And . . . *just take care okay?*" Being instructed of travel cautions by her daughter made her feel like a helpless young kid. Her attention drifted with a gentle tap on her shoulder accompanied with the words," She is calling you." The old lady turned her head and waved a final goodbye.

She was re-adjusting the bag when the girl next to her offered to help. She resisted," *I* . . . will do it. Thanks!" smiling politely hiding a bit of irritation. With a new found determination she pushed the bag that was too stubborn to move into the inadequate space below the seat. Celebrating the little accomplishment she dabbed the beads of sweat with the loose end of her soft, white cotton saree. It had faint prints of blue buds splattered across the white in a systematic fashion that splashed an aura of calmness around the woman. A pair of grey clothed half shoes wrapped her feet in comfort. She looked at her fingers noticing the waves of wrinkles floating on her skin. The oldness struck her and a discomfort spread through her chest. It disturbed her—*how the identity gets erased with age—old woman is how they all define her—no mannerisms, no attributes and no personality! Can I help? That's all they ask. As if incapability was stamped on her face.*

She finally paid attention to the girl sitting next to her, looking at her for the first time. A fashionable haircut with the hair covering half her face was the first thing that caught her notice. A cheerful green t-shirt with a huge red heart at what seemed like an inappropriate location for a print was the second thing. The old lady predicted that pretty soon a pair of music blabbering earphones will be taken out of the girl's bag shutting her off from any possible conversation. She was reminded of her own daughter when in twenties. She turned her face away and stared blankly at the window presuming the young girl wouldn't want to be bothered.

After a little unplanned nap the old woman looked around to figure out where she had reached. Her feet felt tizzy with the constant movement of the train. She turned around to find the girl's face beaming. She was looking at her with a smile. Words were banging through the corners of her lips as if she wanted to talk. She smiled back, little hesitant if she should enquire about the need for a conversation. Noticing her smile the girl spoke with joy and unknown familiarity, "I got short listed for a play!" The old lady was battling on choosing the possible positive reaction. She glanced around to find the usual crowd—some people who were of the similar age of the young girl. She was struck by surprise as to what would have made her—a sixty seven year old lady a part of this unusual conversation. Masking her surprise she extended her hand and conveyed her happiness and best wishes to the girl. The girl talked animatedly about the drama classes and about this big play that was to be staged in front of some reputed actors. The words—so cool, horribly good, incredibly hot, OMG darted in and out of most of her statements but there was never a mention of words like—*old, help or amma*. The old woman had read about the play. Had overheard a conversation about the possible purchase of tickets—she struggled as she responded back trying to match the excitement of the young girl with the handful information she had.

She was being talked to like a *friend*—by a girl who was of the similar age as her daughter. The observation that the girl was almost over a decade younger than her daughter added an additional delight. The next one hour went by with conversations about movies, about artists and the old woman found her herself up to date with each piece of information the girl had to offer. Being a silent spectator to the conversation between her growing and now grown children was the source of this knowledge. She noticed how her words, statements and participation was well received with eagerness by her friend, a young girl, younger, much younger than her daughter. The old lady recollected all the moments when she had willingly extended her presence as someone more comforting like a friend rather than a mother. *There is an age when being the mother to one's own children can be hurtful and not being able to be looked upon as a friend is even more painful.* She had crossed this phase long ago. The hurt had healed. Her children were now grown up man and woman and took utmost care of her well being. Yet she yearned to be included in the discussions they assumed would not suit her—age? What had interest got to do with it? And here she was juggling words with a young thing, in a conversation about the current world—their world, the world her children belong to.

The journey was nearing its end with the Bangalore platform vaguely in sight. The girl pulled out her mobile and asked the old woman's number—to keep in touch. The old lady looked at the screen as she spoke out each number while her eyes matched it with the number that was punched. She was about to say her name, "*Revat . . .* " when she saw the girl type—*Old Aunty—Shatabdi Ex* where her name was supposed to appear—probably with a *aunty* or *Mrs.* tagged along with it. The girl picked up her bags in a hurry, gave a warm hug to the lady. Before dashing towards the door she tucked a piece of paper with her name and number in the old lady's hand as she spoke, "Take care aunty . . . it was very nice meeting you! This is my number."

Revathi's eyes found Ramesh who had made his way into the coach to HELP her—the old mother, the old lady—*the old aunty?*

Later that night along with other discarded belongings of the travellers a tiny unnoticeable piece of paper with a name and number was dumped in the railway trash.

The End

With You—All Along

The light just started to break through the dark. The flickering street lights seemed to cast a magical spell on the roads. The streets lit up and shined golden one moment and turned black cold in the next second. The light bugs had lived their life span and had dropped stiff underneath the street poles. The breeze was cool and serene. Dried fallen leaves playfully rolled with the wind.

Apart from the milkman who silently swooshed past him on his bicycle Aakash didn't spot a single soul. His walk had been complimented with a jump as he hummed a merry tune. There was something nice about having the entire city to him. He stretched his arms and ran like plane on a runway, childish he thought to himself but did it anyway. This was the best part of his day—walking to railway station at four in the morning at boarding the four forty five Memu to Vadodara. He suddenly pulled back his outstretched arms as a light from an apartment interrupted his friendly darkness. Now too cautious of his tall body, moderately built frame he walked like a gentleman.

The following day the light irritated him further. His solo ownership of the early morning was being infringed. He paused a moment to catch the culprit. He felt the curtains slide but assumed it was air and his dreamy eyes still heavy with sleep. The routine followed and curiosity built. He imagined the anger that would engulf him if he finally saw the person switching on that light. He was positive it would be a grumpy little old man too meticulous about picking up the morning milk in person to ensure fine quality. A silhouette cured his curiosity, and surprisingly his anger. Was that a girl? At seventeen he felt excited about the silhouette—unreasonable, he told himself—wishful thinking—and left it at that. After a week the light never switched on.

The alarm blared into ears. Aakriti helplessly tried to place the hand on the snooze but kept missing it. Her eyelids felt burdened by heavy boulders of sleep. She finally slammed the alarm on the floor and kicked herself out the bed after the alarm failed to shut up. She picked it up with a wicked smile and spoke to it," I knew you were good!" and pulled out the batteries. She peered through the window and let the cold air caress her face. She spotted a grown up man or boy swinging as if he were a plane. She couldn't make out the face or the features. Just the outline of a happy young man—is there a possibility he is homeless retard—who feels so happy in the morning? She flipped the light on and pulled a fat book lying in an untouched dusty corner of the study table. She took a week's time to figure out the desire to secure an admission in a good college was nothing in comparison to her desire to have a sound sleep." Let's just say—I am contended with little." she justified herself at the breakfast table in an attempt to convince herself of the decision but publicly announcing it without guilt.

A year later . . .

The room was jam packed. The air was humid with sweat and heavy breath. The uncertainty of the future of thirteen hundred prospective students added a buzz to the room. Announcements from different speakers overlapped and left the worried parents clueless about the procedure. A young lady walked to the main entrance of a local college auditorium. "Queue list one to sixty three—one to sixty three Walk in right now. If you don't report by the time your number is called, you miss the counselling—I repeat—you will miss the counselling". The woman felt exhausted by the first announcement of the day. Her hands already felt sweaty and the crowd would just get worse and worse till the end of the day. As much as she loved working in a college—enjoying the summer breaks she hated the admissions season for obvious reasons. With her last words a part of the impatient crowd stormed through the door and crashed past her as if she was no more needed after the much awaited announcement she made.

"Why can't you decide? You said you want to Computer Science, now what happened?" her father looked confused. Aakriti extended a—you *know how I feel*—look to her mom who had decided to remain silent in the father daughter conversation. "Papa, it is not a good college!" she mumbled. Her father tried his level best to make her decide, "Aah. Listen. If you like sleeping so much young lady—I can tell you a college any better than this is going to do a good job depriving you of it. And it is a decent college." A little drop rolled off her cheek. But she nodded her head in agreement. Her thoughts were interpreted by a loud reprimand.

"I sent you all the way to Baroda. Wonder what you studied there. You didn't clear IIT and now sixty third in line for the admission of a local college. You won't even get computer science. Are you even listening to me . . . ?" Aakash was looking at a girl sitting two rows ahead of him crying? He never understood the fuss girls made about education. Half the girls don't even work after education. They take away the seats of the boys who have no other option but to take up jobs. He smirked and spoke to his father without weighing his words, "Dad, see that girl she is crying . . . ha ha ha . . . She is bloody some thirty ranks ahead of me and she is crying!" His dad screamed in anger, "Oh at least she is crying. You idiot! You have no bloody shame. Eh Shanta? Your son . . . shameless!" She wiped off her tears and shot an angry look at smug, shameless face laughing at her. She quickly and now more confidently proceeded to the next formalities—She wouldn't be an IITian but at least she was better than someone!

4 Years later . . .

Her slender frame was bent like a bow by the luggage she flung on her back. Her white shirt crumpled where the bag met her body and made a random design on her skin. Dragging a trolley bag behind her Aakriti regretted telling her mom," You will come to the station and we both will cry. I am starting to work. It is a new phase. I don't want to cry. You people don't come. I will go by myself." It was like the first breath of independence. She made sure she didn't do anything that her parents did that reasoned why she wouldn't get a coolie to life her bags, why she wouldn't tag along a water bottle from home but buy it here in the train. Her face almost turned blue as she stopped breathing to staunch the smell from making way to her tongue through her nose. The train arrived and she pulled herself together ready for the tussle and tug of war through the door. C1-59 she verified her ticket. A young woman looked at her with a sheepish smile. She was told that the little girl whose nose seemed to be running perpetually, who, disgustingly wiped it off with her tiny finger with a mark of perfect and routine—was her daughter who couldn't travel alone." My seat is C1-03. You are travelling along right? Please make this adjustment from me. "The place already seemed germ infected. The little girl's hands dabbed all over her seat. Aakriti passed a smile with little effort and dumped her luggage at seat no. 3.

"I will call when I reach. I will be fine. You people take care. Now don't delay me or I will miss the train." with these words Aakaash darted his way to his coach from the crowded platform. Worried and loving eyes of his parents lingered on him till he disappeared into the crowd. Though Mr. Sharma never showed the pride he had for the boy the tears that welled up his eyes and a swollen chest gave away his happiness about how the boy has grown and was now on way to make a living for himself, "Eh . . . Shanta . . . my son. Engineer, joining work? Can you believe it?" C-47 Aakaash reached the seat to find it occupied by a couple who clutched their hands as they saw him. He sensed the request he spoke politely making an effort to keep away traces irritation in his voice, "Which is your seat number?" The man explained himself with a sense of urgency," This is my wife. We are travelling together for the first time. My seat no. 2" The stupid smiles of the couple meeting Aakaash's eyes and made his way to the seat before he actually puked!

It was now only a matter of time before conversations weave their way through the awkward recognition of an unpleasant meeting few years ago. A silhouette, dreams of making it to IIT. The placement in the same company, same location—smiles shared, crushes developed and blooming love swept their lives.

P.S: The story had started with the idea of a series of meetings till they grow old. A feeling of, "what could have happened if . . . ," crossed in both of their minds. An affection which cannot be placed as love nor just as familiarity or as infatuation, just the destiny bringing them to together in awkward moments where they support each other without notice. Ah! But, I guess that can't be squeezed in a short fiction. So their lives change and they meet and fall in love. What happens to them later? I'll let the readers unfold it for them in their own thoughts.

The End

Concealing Images

He sat in isolation looking at people around him. The sounds seemed to resonate in the air. He felt a tingling sensation on his back when music flooded through the speakers. His thoughts seemed interrupted as he touched the bridge of his nose in a futile attempt soften the pinch of unfamiliar glasses. Sipping the drink with caution he regained his focus. Every person who entered the bar was caught in his gaze. He looked at them with stark observation and shifted his eyes back to the next person who walked through the door. An unconscious disappointment emerged between slightly pressed lips every time he looked back at the entrance. As if, he tallied each person against a mental description of someone he seemed too eager to meet.

While he observed these people he seemed to know more about them than he wanted to know. Good people trying to be bad. People caught in the company of the bad. Peer pressure, social obligations all became visible to his eyes. He saw women, trading off their dignity to appear little fashionable and broadminded while their inner souls cringed with disgust; men gulping down more drinks than they can handle to reinforce their gender as if someone questioned them about it. Little scum bags killing time till they found someone who wouldn't be able to figure out a few missing notes from their heavy wallets. Bartenders entertaining guests they didn't care about. Everyone masked by concealing identities.

The tiny chips of mirrors on few of the walls transported him back to his school days when he was made to hold two mirrors in front of each other. He remembered the reflections, his astonishment when he looked in to the mirrors—Infinite images. His life seemed to be trapped in the illusion of these infinite images. A sadness wrapped around his heart when he recollected his ten year old self. He couldn't identify with himself anymore and yet he could connect to everybody around him. He had been through everything these people were facing and, a lot more. He felt his hands against his face as if to register how his visage looked like. He caught his image of in one of the reflections—a harmless young man dressed like it was his first visit to the place. The image disturbed him. He shut his eyes and rubbed the back of his neck in an attempt to let go of the emotions that seem to suffocate him. The metallic object tucked at his waist touched his skin and his lips pressed again—disappointment. But this time his eyes didn't have a shade of regret as if this disappointment was embedded to him and had become a part of his life.

The End

A kid, a dad and better toys

"Dad, why are we poor?" this question amazed and saddened his dad. His ten year old son, how did his little life bring him to such a grave question? He pulled the kid up in his arms," What makes you think— we are poor?" The kid hid his face on father's shoulder and mumbled," I don't have many things." Dad laughed in disbelief," Nobody has everything kid!" The kid thought for while and kicked himself out of his dad's arms and sat down on the grass. It is a serious discussion. The message was clear. Dad laid down in the grass beside the kid and asked him," You think that is not true?" The kid looked dejected. "It is true kid. But, it is not a sad thing. It is delightful. Now tell me, what are the things, the absence of which makes you feel poor?"

The kid thought about all the things he craved for," Dad, I don't have the toys the other kids have. I have a tyre, a little rope swing by this tree and a car made out of wooden twigs. They have these vibrant colours and remote controls." Dad smiled," So, do they all have the toys you have and have their toys too?" The kid replied innocently, "No they don't have my toys." "Does that make them poor?" the kid was caught in surprise by this question. "No Dad. They are not." Dad asked him one more question," Aren't you happy when you play with your toys?" The kid couldn't disagree," I am very happy when I play"

"So, you have things few things to play with and you are happy. Those kids have something to play with and they are happy. So why are you poor—kid?" The kid's description of being poor was clear. He spoke confidently, "I think their toys are better than mine". The dad felt a stab in his heart. His son was on the path where many had gone before, comparison. He tried to make his son think about it in a different way, he spoke softly and slowly," So, you are poor because you believe someone has something better than you and not because you don't have what you need." The kid lowered is head and raised a genuine doubt, "But isn't better always good?" The dad replied," Depends on what the better does to you. Will you have more fun? Or will just have one more way to have the fun you were having? Pleasures and joys of living come to us in different ways. We look at others and get dejected when we see how other are getting happiness—fun! But what we forget is we are getting the same happiness and the same fun-just by different means. Now, if both these result in the same outcome—how can one be better and one poor?"

After that there was no conversation. There was no need for one.

The End

Dilapidated

(c) Ashish Arora Photography

She stood amidst all the cacophony but not a sound disturbed her. Her petite frame rested on the bonnet of a dusty grey Alto. Hands folded, perhaps, hugging her—consoling for the years of pain she suddenly felt that the house in front of her, stared back at her. With each step forward she recollected the years she had spent here, assembling them back one by one in her jumbled weak mind. A wave of grief hit her as she climbed the spiral staircase—the rusty handrail rubbed against her white sleeves joining the two cheerful pink floral prints by a tainted brown mark. She stopped and smelt the rust on her sleeve. In the next few minutes she fought her resistance and touched the degenerated steel bar—a feeling of the mixture of cold and dust filled her with welcoming warmth. "I am home! I am home! I am HOME!" she screamed laughing and crying to herself. She entered the house and clung to its walls like worn out plastered paint. Hanging loose but clinging, clinging on to its surface, to all the years, days and moments she had spent here-Her current self attaching to her past through these decrepit walls.

"It's raining!! "She heard a young lady speak nudging playfully at her husband, nestled in a solo worthy piece of furniture—a sofa cum bed bought in a roadside garage sale. And when it began to pour she saw them walk to the window hand in hand, hearing to splitter splatter symphony, of the rain drops that fell into the planned and placed tubs from the gaps in the ceiling. The young lady's hands firmly rested on the sill and his hands rested on hers. His face placed parallel to hers balancing on his chin resting lovingly on her shoulder. She saw the young couple deeply in love as they looked out of the window while it rained a million wishes and dreams.

"Was that me? Was it him?" the sudden flash to the past made her look weaker than she was. Her younger self—full of life and fervour paced across the house going about the mundane chores, as her current lifeless, unexplainably depressed self looked in awe. She shut her eyes trying to remember the day when they moved out. It is strange, how a painful memory can appear like a blur after years, confusing one about the root cause of the pain—leading to pointing fingers at self.

Guilty

I was late again. I expected him to be fuming but I was greeted with a child like smile. The relieved look on his face filled me with guilt of a mother who is late to pick up her kid from the school. I managed to surface a smile quickly occupying the chair opposite him;" You ordered anything?" He shook his head. *Guilt.* The food didn't take much time to arrive. As I mentally fabricated various reasons why I couldn't make it on time he spoke about his day at work, his sister who was spending her last few days in the country, a friend who got promoted, about a walk he took in the morning and about the Gulmohar petals. He suddenly paused. *Guilt.* I was absorbed in my own world and made no effort even to pretend I was listening. I nodded my head and cheerfully added, "Gulmohar petals . . . Interesting!"

A confident young man who once walked up to me and floored me with his charisma, witty remarks and profound insights on everything I did; a man, because of whom I had found sense in the cliché—*feeling complete in love.* Because of whom the restlessness had died out and there was peace. I used to giggle like a little girl in response to his quirky sense of humour and walk with pride as he held my hand at public gatherings. It was a relief knowing I wasn't dating someone stupid. He was respected, was well learned and was in many ways what I believed I liked. I loved. Here he was the same man I had fallen madly in love with-stabbing a piece of baked potato with his fork, fidgeting like a little child restless about not being paid enough attention. What have I done to him?

I suddenly realize there is silence. No conversation. What happened to the Gulmohar petals . . . ? Ask. No. Okay . . . Ask . . . hmmmm," So what about the Gulmohar petals?" A catch his desperate attempt to conceal a smile. I smile and widen my eyes to pretend interest. He continued, "It reminded me of the day when I first saw you. You were standing beneath a Gulmohar tree, with a smile that connected us instantly." *Guilty,* I cut the piece of meat as his words slit my heart. The

162

delicate bands of our relationship strain. How could I forget? Oh . . . He is silent again. Speak something. Anything, "I remember that day!" I bend my lips into a smile. No response. Nothing. He is looking at the food. I feel a sting. Does it matter? I can't think any longer. I am too tired of pretending to care. I liked him. I loved him but I think I ruined him. What if I walk out saying I am bored? Because, there is no other reason, I am just bored. Soaking the bread in the sauce I look at him, still—No response.

Suddenly, I catch his jet black eyes staring right at me. Wait. He has a smile on his face. I am missing something. I try to mute my thoughts and reel back every word he said,—the Gulmohar petals. I look at him and smile stupidly I am missing something. Something, What? I smile wider in an attempt to make him speak. But nothing. Arrgh. Stubborn young man. My eyes dart to something red on the table. Oh Gulmohar petals. I reach out and pick them. He holds my hand. I am confused. He is still smiling. Oh God! Speak something. Mute. My thoughts go blank. I can't think anything. I am still smiling as I don't know how I am supposed to emote feeling *nothing*. Say something. Something. "I love you!" he finally speaks. I feel trapped. I try to react," I love . . . hmmm. Thank you!" I see his smile fade. **Guilty**.

Saturday, July 16, 2011

"Okay easy.. one step at a time"

"Okay easy.. one step at a time.. you will be fine" she could almost picture that scene. She was a little girl and she felt her sponge feet land on the ground and she suddenly stretched out her hands in a final attempt to balance and thud she landed on her bum and burst out into a cry. When you are a two year old you just cry for evident reasons. You fell on the floor hit your tiny bottom and that made you cry. That cry was not for the inability to walk. The cry was the fear of experiencing the same pain if you attempt the same activity again. She felt two soft hands rub against her cheeks wiping out the tears. And she heard," Okay easy.. one step at a time.. you will be fine"

As she walked along the wide spread magnificent beach she felt like a little girl again. This sudden memory of the early childhood seemed to fit into her current life—real well not as a little girl but as a young adult. "Okay easy.. one step at a time.. you will be fine". A smile spread across her lips as that line played on her mind.

A beach walk was a remedy to fix her gloomy days, an attempt to throw away her worrisome thoughts into the water and watch them sink. Was she trying everything too early? Too hard or too fast?? Nothing grave happened. But there were so many plans and no priority chart. It was a war between fulfilling fancy wishes and becoming a sensible grownup. It was like army of things to do, things to buy, things to save. One step forward meant moving an army ahead. And every cancelled, postponed plan felt like one army man dead or injured. Injury was similar to that thud when she was learning to walk. Should she cry? Instead she laughed. Looked at the waves . . . rushing towards the shore. Crest by crest. Step by step. She walked and it played again on her mind, "Okay easy.. one step at a time.. you will be fine"

P.S: If they story appears little vague—it was a deliberate effort.

Thursday, July 7, 2011

My Smile

Anger—is always considered as a negative emotion. It probably is. But I find it incredibly powerful unlike the common belief that the one that gets angry loses the battle. There is immense strength in knowing in a second you couldn't care enough to rip a person apart either in words or otherwise and you are holding back yourself because of a thin line of thought which tells you not to. There is immense strength when that line is stretched, tested time and again and you are pushed against it almost making way through it but bouncing back to safety region way below its limit of elasticity. There is immense power in that tolerance in that control you have while maintaining a clam exterior while you are molten and burning inside. There is remarkable amount of pleasure to smile at a person you almost have the urge to engage in a once for all battle with. Smile and built that tension. That has an effect of sharpening one's knife before a ghastly battle. Just that empowering feeling in knowing the damage you can but will never cause.

I held it all close. Not letting a drop of emotion spill. For fourteen years. I just smiled. Smiled at that one person-irrespective of what he did, irrespective of the unjustified emotional wounds that have left my soul in tatters. There was just one day when he felt his words and actions wouldn't suffice—he decided to leave an imprint of his hand on my cheek—unjustified again. I gripped his hand right in the middle of the air. I looked at him and I smiled. It gave a satisfaction that people who fight back don't know. He got the message. I wouldn't let him win. He kept poking words, abuses beautifully wrapped in sarcastic comments and public embarrassments over years in front of people from all walks of life and people of all kinds. But I just smiled.

Today he is reduced to manic trying all sorts of tactics to undo what cannot be undone. He has failed his innumerable attempts to prove it was all in my mind. He has failed at fooling himself and me that life was always normal. And he failed to understand that the darkest walls I built around myself will never break. He has failed. And Me? I smile. My smile has undergone a million alterations, has undergone various shades of expressions—suppressed anger, happiness of being invincible and lot more that cannot be explained but can only be felt. Today my smile emerges from the confusion and desire I have managed to create in his head and that new definition of being powerless that is visible in his eyes. From that words that leave his lips as abuses but fall on my ears like a purrs of a lost injured cat. It emerges from being able to look right into his eyes and see him breaking. It emerges from the indomitable strength I have found in resistance. It emerges from still being able to be myself around other people.

I have been complimented enough about my smile from people who do not have a clue about the deep dark emotional labyrinths I walked through. People figure it out in their own ways and assign attributes to my personality. They tell me my smile is charming. And what can I say? I just smile. And this smile breaks into a chuckle and now a laugh!

The End

Two Houses

I sweep the roads on the 19th Cross—Everyday. I have been doing this for 18 years now. In the initial years of my work the roads fascinated me. Call me crazy but I developed a sense of belonging to wide tar sheets running on the earth. Every morning I walked to my roads to see which flower, which tree has knocked on its doors and left its traces while I was asleep someplace else. The road had a story to tell. Every day I would fix the puzzle as I swept the remains, throwaways and imagine what could have happened the previous day. I felt like an investigator scrutinizing a crime scene to retrace the paths of people who have been on these roads. The only difference was—people always left their belongings unlike the actual trespassers who take things away.

While this fascination for roads—is exciting. I couldn't help but discover how non-existent my presence was to the people who lived here—the 19th cross. They were unaware how much I could tell about their lives just by looking at their balconies. By—catching the glimpse of their lives once in a while. It is strange—the power of human comprehension. I will tell you the story of two houses—two balconies in particular.

It was 5 a.m. and I saw the balcony light go on in one of the houses that stood next to each other on the one, two three . . . yeah the fourth floor. Every house was identical in that building. I saw a young lady walkout. The balcony was beautifully decorated, brought to life by small crotons, few flowers and creepers that gave the icy grills of the balcony—welcoming warmth. The lady ran her hands on the plants. She looked at the early morning. She had a beautiful smile. I fell in love with her happiness. It is amazing how people can have that effect on you. Her smile made me smile. She went back in for her regular coffee (I suppose). Over few days of observation I figured out in five minutes, the husband would be there repeating the same actions with a coffee mug in his hand. I loved his happiness too.

Every day at 5.30 a.m. I walk by that street to collect the heaps of dried leaves I leave while sweeping. And that day and all the other days that followed I saw the light on the other balcony go on. A woman with a grumpy little face stormed into the balcony. The balcony was lined with buckets of all sizes and the grill supported the mopping cloths torn from old clothes. She picked up a broom from the balcony floor, threw the mopping cloth into one of the buckets and slammed the door behind her back. I could tell there was a husband though I never saw him—as the torn cloth pieces seemed to be a part of worn out shirts.

Standing here on the ground—levels below their lives I don't know the intricate details of what happens to them every day. But all I understand is—two families probably in same financial status. Living in the same houses, same locality, similar jobs probably—how different they were. One balcony full of happiness and life the other too caught in the mundane activities not a moment to smile. Could it be perspectives? I believe it is.

The End

The Unusual—Part1

Her eyes fixed on the television screen-following the heartbeat flashing on the ECG of patient Rohnda being treated by Dr. Douglas in ER. She felt sadness rush through her heart. Her face fell. The dinner she was enjoying till now was left cold. Before she realized the episode ended. On a good day she would have had a wonderful time watching her favourite show, would have slept with a smile with the crazy dialogues running through her head at times making their way into her dreams resulting in waking up with a smile.

Dr. Douglas was as charming as ever. But, today she bluntly switched off the television. Her eyes painted the heartbeat right in front of her as if they were fixed on her vision like viewing through a funky glass affixed before her twin eyeballs. The tiny crests, the high, the low, the little jumps and little falls—the heart beats. A faint smile surfaced on her lips. She pulled out a piece of paper and drew a horizontal line across it. She put a dot below it. Suddenly feeling tired she snuggled under her rug after switching off the lights. Beneath shut eyelids she tried to process a reason for this abysmal low she felt. She smiled again at the irony—how she shut off the lights in these strange dark nights and looked for answers. Before she could decide the reason sleep had won the battle over thoughts and her mind shutdown into a dreamless slumber.

Next morning—she looked at the piece of paper. She saw the little dot below the line. She took a bite of the ginger toast, sipped in some coffee and spent a few seconds before she drew the path of a plane take off right from the dot above the line that cut the sheet into two equal halves. She tried to figure out a reason again. But morning time was way too demanding to be invested in crazy little thoughts. So, brushing aside everything she rushed over the hectic schedule for the day. She knew she would get back to it in the evening rather for few more evenings.

Thursday, June 30, 2011

The Unusual—Part2

That evening as she drove back from office-she figured out she was comfortably ahead of her so called life plan. For a woman of twenty six she had fair share of investments, a stable job, independent and healthy (*touchwood*) parents and a very loving relationship with her boyfriend. He was suave, matured, well settled and had enough charm to keep her constantly amused. "Didi . . . Do phool lelo na didi. (Please buy few flowers)" She zapped back from deep thoughts that refused to elude her. "Nahi . . . Acha..dus ke phool de do (No . . . okay give me flowers for ten rupees)." After momentary distraction at the traffic signal driving on the silken road she nudged her brain cells—Nothing. Nothing.Nothing. Arrghhhhhhh! She shook her head as if affirming the emptiness of her mind and suddenly calmed down.

Climbing up to the fourth floor she smiled at everyone who passed by making friendly little chats on her way. She rushed and shut the door stood in front of a mirror. "Am I happy?" Her lips instantly bent into a smile and her eyes lit up. Yeah! Hell Yeah! She rummaged around the breakfast table and picked up that paper. She drew a sharp upward slant followed by series of bumps. "Am I sad?" Her hand refused to move. She reluctantly scribbled few lows on the paper. She left the pencil on the table—let it roll over its flat surface and hit the floor breaking its nib.

Chilled water bounced off her skin as she splashed it against her face. In few seconds a layer of white foam covered her features. She popped open her eyes to catch her image in the mirror. She smiled at the snowman bauble staring back at her—hanging above the mirror. Her refection felt same. The smile broadened. She put on her best top and headed out for dinner. She was sensuous, intelligent and carried herself with an unmatched grace. She unlocked the door ran back in for a moment grabbed the paper piece and shoved it in her purse.

Spreading it out with her palm she ironed the folded piece of paper on the table carefully placing it in the dry area between the moist rims

170

of table cloth at the base of the wine glasses. He smiled at her—"What is this . . . ? A coded love note with a heart beat?" He waited for her to respond but she didn't. Instead, she had that *I figured it all smile!* He was very familiar with that smile. Back in their early courtship days—he would see her swing up and down for inexplicable reasons. Putting off scheduled dates, getting lost in between conversations . . . He had almost concluded her to be uninterested in the relationship or too delusional. But just when his irritation would reach its brink she would pace in with a bundle of energy and tell him the most wise explanation connecting life. He had eventually learned that she was *unusual* and her *I figured it all smile!* meant something interesting was coming up. He smiled back.

She waited for his initial thoughts to process and die out. She wanted a clean slate to present what she had found. "Okay here you go!" she paused and cleared her throat. "Can you answer a few simple questions?" He raised his glass in response and clinked!

The Unusual—Part3

"What are we doing with our lives? We are striving hard to reach a state of balance—A mental state of no disturbance, a consistency—say— of constant happiness. "Correct?" he nodded in response. "A balance—a state of constant happiness—unbelievable—what we are striving for, but, yeah true." She proceeded," So, we are busy ironing the little folds in our lives. Trying hard to do things correct, Feel good, Feel Nice, Feel Happy?" He replied, "Well, yeah it is a healthy sign. Anyone who isn't doing that is in serious danger." She smiled," Interesting. So you being the well learned, fairly mature man you are—balanced if I may add. Do you feel that constant state of happiness? I know every tiny bit of you and neither you nor I or we have grave problems plaguing our lives. Are we too balanced? Too achieved or accomplished to be hit by any emotion?" She had managed to strike a chord. He thought for a while. She thought too.

After few minutes of no conversation, he said, "No!" shaking his head, "Not at all! I feel low for unknown reasons. At times I feel I have lost the meaning of what happiness is. I am doing well. Doing well, I am in love. I love my job. Each day I get up and do what I feel like. But, at times that constant happiness that constant high is confusing." She clapped her hands with excitement," Ahha! Yes!! The 'constant'—let's take that word and replace it with 'balance'—That balance is confusing! It is that need and effort to achieve balance that is ironically creating these incomprehensible thoughts? I wonder which category would that fall into—high—low—little ups, little downs."

She tapped her finger on the paper and traced it along the lines that resembled a heartbeat. "This—is a heartbeat. It is life. It is our life, yours, mine, and everyone's life. We all are alive for this pulsating, vibrating rhythmic and constant up and down. Highs and lows in our hearts, the core of our human existence. "She pulled out a pen and drew a flat line cutting across the heartbeat. She tapped her pen at that start of the line as she spoke "This line is what we are trying to achieve, A balance—A constant. What happens when the heartbeat is flat? What does it mean? It means death. It means no life. Balance kills us in different ways we are not capable of understanding. We need to vibrate, to resonate with the life. We need to move high, move low. When do we feel something? When there is a deviation from what is already there. So we need to go off balance to feel good—one cannot constantly feel good. One has to have high and low. Little ups little downs. And then the heart—4beats and pumps life into our mechanical bodies. We resonate, we pulsate, we vibrate we are living. We are happy, yet little sad. But we are happy."

She looked at him to understand if she was going too fast. She was happy to notice him smile. He said, "So to sum it up my darling *unusual* girl. You say—It is okay if I am sad. It is okay if I am thrown off the balance. I don't need to struggle. For I feel sad just because I am alive. It is a part of living. And I am sad because I cannot constantly feel happy. I will hit a low because of that constant happiness and there will be another transition. The transition will cause the happiness again. And these transitions will happen every time. That is what I was born with. That is what gave me life." She nodded with the smile of a child. Her struggle, her thoughts, her highs, her lows for the past two days mapped on a piece of paper resembled the heartbeat. Her heart beat, her life. She picked up the pen and signed "*With love, Your Unusual. P.S. Coded love note*". She slipped it in the pocket over his heart and winked as she said, "Keep this with you."

THE END

P.S: The story is very unusual. It is not a love story. It is not a story about pain. It is not like any other story that would have read. But in the end it does have something to convey.